A Mended Vessel

A Mended Vessel

PEARL K. McCULLOUGH

To order additional copies of this book, contact:
Xlibris Corporation
1-888-795-4274
www.Xlibris.com
Orders@Xlibris.com
67224

DEDICATION

A Mended Vessel is dedicated to my dear Granny,
whose love was never ending, and to my three daughters:
Melba Crouch-Kubat, Sandra Sorensen, and Tobie Praus.
They kindled a fire in my heart that gave strength to my frailties,
like the spider web and chimney soot that
Granny used to stop the bleeding many years ago.

They have been an asset in mending my broken vessel,
erasing hate, fear and desperation, and healing wounds
that for so long were open and bleeding.

ACKNOWLEDGMENTS

I WOULD LIKE to acknowledge Marnie Sperry, whose help is greatly appreciated, and my husband Mack, who has been endearing and patient while I worked long hours finishing this book.

Also, Michael McCullough, my stepson, who insisted that I finish this book.

FOREWORD

I AM AN 86-year-old woman who struggled my entire life with difficult memories of my time as a child, as an adult and now as a mature woman. As I reread pages of this book I felt must be written, I ask only that you as a reader keep an open mind and heart and read with eyes of understanding and compassion as you see me in my nakedness, hiding nothing from you.

If I had all these years to live over again, would things be the same? I have asked myself this question time and time again and each time I am drawn back to the first memory of my life, as I have known it.

So to the many tutors I have had throughout the years, I owe you so much. You have given me hope, taught me to be patient, and last, but not least, you, like my beloved Granny and Aunt Hat, have encouraged me to continue drinking from the cup of knowledge.

I seek neither revenge nor justification for the happenings in my life. Time has passed and I have dealt with the issues appearing herein. I now am closely acquainted with peace and contentment. The tears are few, the nightmares are quieter and my days are long and fruitful.

I liken my life to an earthen vessel, shattered through mistreatment and mishandling. It has taken many years to mend this vessel to make it once again strong and worthy of holding enough love and compassion for myself and for others.

In this book, *A Mended Vessel*, I have tried to protect the innocent (some names have been changed to ensure anonymity) while offering encouragement to women not to accept defeat, to know that there is strength within to help get through difficult times. Never stop trying.

Always love yourself, and then you will be able to love others so that they can accept and love you in return.

I will go on doing the many things required of me as I grow older while being rocked in the cradle of love and devotion by family and friends.

PEARL K. MCCULLOUGH

CHAPTER 1

My Earliest Years

I AM TOLD I was born on a warm summer's night in June 1923, in my home in the mountains of North Carolina. My birth is recorded in the Hall of Records in Sunburst in that state. Dr. Stringfellow in Blowing Rock, North Carolina, delivered me, assisted by a friend of my mother's, an Indian lady from Cherokee. My maiden name is Pearl Katherine Gilbert.

I've been told that even at my birth, my tiny hands made fists that I held high in the air, and my loud voice drowned out my mother's exhausted weeping.

We were seven children in our family. There had been nine, but the two first-borns, twins, died at eighteen months and two years old, both of whooping cough. I was next to the youngest. I remember my mother standing over our beds and telling us to say our prayers, sometimes with her hand on our heads. She spoke softly, as if to herself or perhaps to God, and she spoke of Him often to all of us. Yes, she was the mother of nine children, eighteen months between the ages of each.

Mother was of small frame, five feet one inch tall. Her weight was never over 110 pounds. She died in her early forties. I recall this as if it were yesterday. Several nights before she passed, she had my sister Lucille, the oldest, line all of us up near her bed, and she told us a beautiful story of a mother that had a group of children entrusted to her care. How she loved and cared for these little ones! But she found to her surprise she must go away and would not see them for a while. She was to leave them in the care of their guardian angel, so they would be in the best of hands. The story was so beautiful, and we children later talked of it often, and each of us have remembered it all our lives.

We were not allowed in our mother's room after that. Our dad told us Mother was very ill, and we were quiet and tiptoed around the house, knowing something was very wrong. After some days, our father gathered us together and told us Mother was in heaven.

That loving, gentle person who graced our lives was laid to rest on a hillside in a settlement in Tom's Creek, Virginia. I remember the day of her funeral was dark and gray, and it rained. I recall stepping in puddles of water as we walked down the hillside to the cars below. I was just six years old at that time. That is how I remember Mother.

Mother did not have a headstone at that time because, we were told, during those depression times Dad could not afford one because he had lost everything. Fifty years later, however, my brother Edd and I returned to that place, now called Sandy Ridge, and placed a marker on her grave. We looked out over the mountain and saw where all the trees had been cut or pushed down as the strip mines crept up the mountainside, but the ten or so acre parcel of land set aside for the cemetery had been untouched. I thought, "Mother, you too have a guardian angel."

*　　*　　*

I learned at a very early age that children were to be seen but not heard. I guess from the beginning, having made up my mind to change several things, I started with this one thought in mind: I *would* be heard!

The birds, bees and all the wild things listened to me, if for no other reason than because they were in a state of shock at the sight of a frail, motherless child singing as loud as her voice would allow, or crying softly as wind in the lovely pine trees whispered words only a child with no love and tenderness shown her could ever understand.

This was my world for the first two years following my mother's death. I dared not allow anyone to enter here nor break the wall I had spent so much time building around my outer self in order to protect my inner self.

With my loving mother no longer in my life, I longed to be loved by my father, Harrison Gilbert, to be held in his strong arms or rocked gently on his knee. This, however, was just not the mountain way in which I was raised, and I was a "bad" child to think one needed this type of affection. I learned from my father that anyone who thinks in such a fashion turns out bad. The frustration I felt caused me to feel that every rule my father made was waiting to be broken as soon as I could get around to doing so.

My father told the girls in our family that women brought unpleasant things on themselves by the way they acted. Good women don't hang around men. They keep to themselves, do household chores, raise children, and are good wives and mothers. I was in constant fear of doing the wrong thing, and when I did, I was never given the chance to explain my actions. I was sure I would never earn my father's trust or love regardless of what I did.

We were forbidden to talk while at the table for a meal. We were told as young girls not to cross our legs, wear pants, shorts, or even dresses that were the least bit tight, as that was unacceptable to our father. My father was in complete control at all times, and he ruled his household with an iron hand. Perhaps he was reared like this. I wanted so much to love this giant of a man, but he was always beyond my reach and understanding.

I can see now that my father did not intend to hurt me; he only wanted me to learn to be strong and not lean on others. He was brought up without love and he survived, and since I was of his own flesh and blood, I too would survive. Poor Dad! This was how he thought we children should be raised. The love denied me by my father would have meant so much to me.

After Mother died and Dad moved the family to Monarch, Virginia, our brother Edd was the real stabilizing factor in our lives. My younger brother James was four years of age, I was six, Mary eight, Dora ten, Pauline twelve, the oldest sister Lucille was fourteen, and Edd was sixteen.

Due to the circumstances of that time in our country, our father (like so many others) had lost everything—home, property, and his job as overseer of a large coal mine in Tom's Creek, Virginia. Edd told us Father was not well, so he was taking us to live with other family members until Father was better. Edd promised all of us he would come for us within a year.

My sister Mary and I went to live with our aunt and uncle in South Carolina and the other kids were sent to North Carolina. Being separated was very hard. However, our dear brother Edd did what he said, and cared for us in so many ways. He gave us the hope of our family coming together again.

After one year, Edd arrived in a small Model A Ford and took Mary and me home to Virginia. I remember we got to ride in the car's small rumble seat. (A rumble seat is a small seat located where the car's trunk normally would be. It opened from the front to the rear of the car, forming a back cushion, and there was a second cushion to sit on.)

We learned upon returning home that our dear brother had gone to work in the coal mines so he could help our father bring all of us together again as promised. Edd was then nearly seventeen years old. I was seven, full of questions of the type most seven-year-olds would ask—everything going on in life, the mines, the people, school, why things had happened as they did, etc., but there were few answers to be had.

PEARL K. MCCULLOUGH

However, we had all arrived and were together again, and life went on as we settled into our home in the mining camp. I started school in Monarch, Virginia at a school within walking distance of our house, and I was in first grade. I was behind since I'd been unable to start school at six, and Edd helped me catch up during that first year. I have since relied on his advice and judgment for years, and have respected and loved him our entire lives. I could never find words to express my love and appreciation to my dear older brother. I tried hard in later years to convey my feelings of gratitude, and I pray that he understood.

CHAPTER 2

The Coal Mines

OUR COUNTRY WAS in a depression at that time, and our president, Mr. Roosevelt, introduced us to his New Deal Program. This program was to lift our country from its knees to an upright position. It would take time and effort on everyone's part. Coal from the mines was important to our country's economy, and once Mrs. Roosevelt even came to the mines and spoke to the workers.

I recall watching as this gracious lady asked the miners to please not leave their jobs, as many were returning to the farms. "There will be better times," she stated. "Let's work together. We can and will survive and will be stronger." I cheered along with hundreds of others, and we welcomed the thought of better times.

As we were turning to leave, Mrs. Roosevelt asked to be taken into the mines. As the crowd watched in disbelief, the wife of the president of this great country seated herself in a motorcar used to pull small coal gondolas from the mines, and rode into the tunnel of Monarch Mines, quietly saying, "Let's go forward." And we did just that.

At his new job, my father became very involved with rights of the coal miners. Although I was very young, I recall watching and listening when he spoke to the miners. Paraphrasing his talks, this is what I remember:

"Men of our country, I have been thinking. We are tall in our stature, but short on brainpower. We are working for such low wages, most of us with little or no education and no promise of improvements from the mine owners. When I was an overseer I was told repeatedly, 'Take good care of the mules that pull the coal gongs from the mines. Mules are hard to replace, but men can take care of themselves, and are to be found anywhere and everywhere, and at a much lower cost to the mining company.'

"I am going out on a limb for you and your families. Stand with me. When I call for a strike, pick up your tools and walk out of the mines. If you do not, you will be carried out. If you live and continue to work you will be called a 'scab', meaning you are nonunion. The union dues are small, the risk is great, but the time is now, and you have an invitation to become a member of The United Mine Workers of America. Fall in line to my right and sign this form, pay your dues for the first month beginning today, and become a member! If you are unable to pay now, the Union will pay them for you."

There were many strikes, much work stoppage, and sometimes they lasted for months until the mine owners and miners could agree or address a problem. The mining companies were finally brought to their knees, and many workers said, "This is what we should have done years ago."

When the men were called out on strike the union brought in food for the workers. It was often late in arriving, though, so farmers shared food with the miners' families. I recall seeing bags of food that had been left on our porch in the early morning hours. We never knew the names of those who had shown us this kindness. We were grateful and shared our bounty with others. I was about six and a half or seven years of age about this time.

My sisters, Lucille and Pauline, took to overseeing the house and children and never did return to school. They prepared all the meals and washed laundry at least once a week, though we did not have many clothes. They kept the house, did the buying of food as needed, and cared for the family. We each helped with chores depending on our size and age. Some jobs were small and some larger and more difficult, but we did them. We became aware early in life that togetherness was important, and we religiously maintained this commitment and teamwork in order to create a lasting bond.

Mary and Dora had the job of bringing in coal for the heating and cooking fires. The coal yard was nearby, but the coal was heavy. They carried it in coal buckets that were not very big, so many trips were required to fill the coal bins. I often helped carry small lumps of coal in a sand bucket. At first they complained about the hard work, but later they enjoyed filling the bins, even laughing and calling themselves "firewomen". I had a child's broom, and my main job was to sweep the porches and walkway, which I did several times a day because I felt so pleased they had given me a job to do.

My youngest brother, James, was restless and wanted to be doing something every moment, so we all took turns looking out for him. Lucille was so concerned that James would fall and hurt himself that she always had someone keep a watchful eye on him during his daily runs around the house and yard. In spite of our careful watchfulness, though, one day he did fall from the porch and broke his arm. Lucille did not let us forget this incident for several months.

Food was scarce during the Depression, and we ate lots of beans and dried foods. The farmers nearby had fruit trees, and the fruit was cheap. We often picked apples ourselves, and wild grapes grew everywhere. They were called fox grapes, not as sweet as one would want, but they were edible. Berries called huckleberries by the miners were plentiful. There were wild blueberries, and my sisters made pies and jelly from those as well as from crabapples.

We enjoyed these tasty morsels all summer and into early winter, and sometimes we even roasted them on a stick in an open fire in the back yard. All of the young folk gathered to roast apples or sweet potatoes, or just sat around. This was a common sight in those days of togetherness.

PEARL K. MCCULLOUGH

CHAPTER 3

The Kind, Bad Man

AT THE TENDER age of eight, the first of a long line of sorrows and problems began for me when an older man in our community began to notice me. He gave me sweets, sat me on his knee, and rocked me gently in his strong arms as I had so often longed for my father to do.

Not for one moment did I realize what was happening until it was too late. I remembered how my father had warned me that wanting to be caressed was wrong, but I didn't understand what he meant or how he meant it or what could happen next. Instead, I felt I was just plain bad for having such needy feelings.

A terrible thing happened to me at the school in this little village of Monarch in the mountains of Virginia. This teacher, who taught the seventh grade, was the man responsible for the rude awakening of this eight-year-old child who did not know the difference between a father's desperately needed love, and sex, which I knew nothing about. This man was a pillar of the community, and he had a wife and family.

This teacher, who I will call Mr. Roberts, often asked me to stay after school to beat out the erasers or wash the blackboard, and this gave me a feeling of being a part of things. I felt happy to be near this warm, fatherly man. He talked to me as we walked in the woods, and told me many things of the outside world. He told me how he would like to take me into his home, so I would have a real family. In Mr. Roberts, I saw the devoted father figure I so longed for. I felt my dreams could become a reality!

On the last day of school this kindly, gentle man told me to stay, that he had something to tell me. I was not to tell anyone I was staying because the two of us were to have a birthday party. I never had a birthday party in all my eight years, so this alone was enough to make me want to keep this secret. Mr. Roberts had brought sandwiches and pawpaws (a fruit that even today makes me violently ill whenever I see it).

We ate, and then he started playing ball with me. First he threw the ball to me and I would catch it and throw it back. After awhile the ball was thrown so hard I couldn't reach it. After about four throws, the ball rolled beneath the school building.

I was afraid to crawl under the dark building, so I wanted to leave the ball. But Mr. Roberts spoke very firmly to me and called me a "scaredy cat". He offered to go under the building with me to help me find the ball. I asked to wait outside, but he acted as though I had hurt his feelings by not wanting to go under the building with him, and he said he would go first. I handed him a long hickory stick to beat down the cobwebs.

Mr. Roberts held my hand very tightly and pulled me along with him to the middle of the building. There, with the cold spiderwebs slapping my face and the dust of the years bearing witness, he removed my clothes with such force that my undergarments were in shreds. When the pain of the unmerciful rape was so bad I could no longer endure it, he told me to bite down on the very stick I had given him to remove the cobwebs.

Mr. Roberts was weeping when he left me alone beneath the building. I was so stunned I couldn't move. After two hours, I crawled from under the building and ran into the outside toilet, and there I stayed until it was dark and I could go home. I went into the bedroom I shared with two of my sisters, and I stayed there for the next three weeks, too sick to even speak. I realize now

PEARL K. MCCULLOUGH

that I was in a state of shock. I remember feeling so ashamed, as if I did something wrong to cause this to happen.

My father came to see me only twice during this time, and my sisters brought me food that I was unable to eat. Finally the doctor was summoned, and he came, reeking of whiskey. When he tried to examine me I screamed and fought him until he finally just told my father I had stomach cramps and leg pains (what he called "growing pains"). I'm sure it never occurred to him that I had gone into the very pit of hell and was too terrified to tell anyone about it. For many months thereafter I spoke to no one, and finally my father started to think something was wrong with my mind. My sisters were concerned for me and brought me food and watched over me, but of course, they didn't know what had happened and did not understand why I was feeling as I did.

When school started again I was too sick to attend. I saw to this myself by chewing bitterweed and also a weed called rabbit tobacco, so I could keep my stomach upset. I would have died rather than go back to that school! I would have been in the second grade at the time, and this ended up being the end of my public school education.

At home, my father had always insisted that we had books to read. As we sat in the living room every night, it wasn't easy for me to hold a book in my small hands and sit up straight in a high-backed chair just to please him. Everyone must be doing something. Time was not to be wasted at our house, so I sat night after night with the book, *The Little Red Hen,* opened in my lap, while I stared off into space.

After some time I took matters into my own hands. As often as the books were opened and placed in my lap, I quietly closed them and merely stared into the fire. I sat for hours on end as if frozen. Everyone wondered what was to become of this strange girl of Harrison's who wouldn't talk and was afraid of everyone.

Father went to his death unaware of what Mr. Roberts had done to me. I understand now that my father was acting the only way he knew how, but the pain, guilt, and frustration I carried for so many years added greatly to the hatred I felt for him. Somehow, I felt he should have understood, should have known what had happened to me, should have known how to care for me, protect me, and avenge me! My burden was so heavy that several times during my life I collapsed under its extreme pressure. Only time and God's love were able to release me from this terrible struggle to finally begin mending myself. It was if I was a broken vessel, first cracked and then shattered into many pieces by the painful and traumatic events of my young life. There were so many questions I could not answer myself: Was I to blame? Was I wrong to want my father's love and tenderness? What had I done to provoke what happened to me? I have asked myself these questions over and over again for many years and the answers as yet wait to be found.

PEARL K. MCCULLOUGH

CHAPTER 4

I Go To Live With Granny

AFTER ALMOST SIX months of this silence on my part, my sister Lucille, then about sixteen, wrote to my Granny, our mother's mother, in North Carolina by way of Aunt Fern, my mother's sister, telling her to please come, that something had happened to me, that I could not talk, and Father planned to send me to a mental hospital. Our father believed I was mentally ill, and he could not take care of me. The company doctor was gathering information to have me placed in a hospital near Richmond, Virginia. Lucille, crying, had told my father she would care for me, to no avail.

But then my grandmother, Alice Gregory, arrived from North Carolina. She seemed a strange person in voice and manner, but there was something about her that made me want to trust her. She brought herb teas that she gave me, and she also gave me love, which by that time I was unable to respond to.

Granny had much advice for my father regarding his responsibility to his other children. I overheard them talking one night of his plans to place me in a home for the "feebleminded." My father's words were harsh and hurtful, and they fell hard on the heart of a young child touched by the death of her mother, abused by an adult she had trusted, and was now to be cast aside by an unloving and uncaring father. Why was this happening to me?

That night when the house was quiet and dark, trembling with fright, I crept into my grandmother's room and crawled into her bed. With my father's words ringing in my ears "females bring bad things upon themselves," I clung to Granny all night, and when dawn arrived, she awakened my father and told him I did have awareness of what was going on around me.

So in the end, I left my father's house when I was eight years old, and I went to live with Granny. There I did not feel so badly about not talking. For two years I spent many happy hours playing on the beautiful mountainside, walking along dusty roads, or sitting on the creek bank with my feet in the cold mountain stream. I watched the wild things and saw the freedom with which they moved, like the glorious butterflies fluttering about, or a moth as he pumped up his wings after having freed himself from the prison of his cocoon. Perhaps I, too, could free myself from my cocoon. Instinctively, I knew I must be patient and bide my time. I held my secret to my heart and kept the outside world out, for this was now my world. I maintained my silence. My wall was secure.

Granny's house was as kind and gentle as that sweet, patient person abiding within its walls. It was built atop a lovely mountain near Max's Patch Mountain, and the first time I saw it I remember thinking what loving hands must have pieced that house together with such care and concentration, because each room added on had a different personality, as if many hands had played a part in the formation of its walls.

This house was old and blended in well with the mountains. On a gray day when the fog drifted over Max's Patch Mountain, the old home took on the same shade, and from a distance one had to look closely to see it.

Granny's cabin had white pine floors that were scrubbed with a corn-shuck broom once a week to keep them clean. She used a long stick about the size of today's broomstick and a piece of board with a dozen or so holes in it. She ran a corn-shuck into each hole, and then the broomstick was inserted into the center hole. The broom was dipped into hot water with lye soap in it and pushed back and forth until the floor was thoroughly scrubbed. A large bucket of cold water from the well was used to rinse the floor. We used a piece of sheepskin to take the water up, and then put the furniture back into place. When all was clean and in perfect order, we went on to the next room.

Each Friday, we went into the forest and cut three or four pieces of brush as tall as our heads and tied them together, and we used these to sweep the yard until it was neat and tidy. We even cleaned underneath the house at least once a month. Granny's home wasn't closed in and stood two or three feet above the ground. There were shutters on most of the windows and a part of the house had glass windows. Some of the roof was tin. Granny told me that once the roof had caught fire and the neighbors replaced it with tin.

I liked the house. The rain beat a merry tune on its firm top, and I felt snug and safe within its strong walls.

Granny's home had a large kitchen, an even bigger parlor, two bedrooms on each side of the house, and two other rooms that Granny called "the shed rooms." Both the kitchen and the parlor had large fireplaces. This was the only heat in the house, but I never remember being cold. I do recollect, however, that Granny put two flat stones in the fireplace in the evenings, wrapped each of them in a cloth, and put one at the foot of each of our beds to warm our feet. The fire was banked with a great log at night, the fireguards put firmly into place, and the braided rugs were pulled back a safe distance from any flying sparks or burning embers that might shoot forth once the house had settled for the night.

Granny's beds had shuck mattresses that were made by the ladies in the mountains. The shucks had been torn apart and placed in a sewn cover, leaving one end open, so in the fall the shucks could be changed. The dried shucks made a nice rustling noise when I turned in bed. Their fresh, clean smell would cling to my nostrils as I drifted off to sleep as if on a cloud.

We each slept atop a large feather bed that was placed on top of the mattresses, and these we aired and sunned as often as weather permitted. I remember making these beds with such care. The first thing we did upon arising was to pull the covers back and fling open the shutters so fresh air could enter the bedrooms. Once they had ample time to air, we made the beds. The feather bed needed to be folded in half and beaten with much force, then turned on the other side and beaten again to fluff up the feathers. Then it was straightened on the bed and a broom handle was used to smooth out the mounds of feathers. After running the broom handle up and down the bed a few times, it took on the likeness of a new-mown meadow, raked and put in order.

PEARL K. MCCULLOUGH

CHAPTER 5

Granny's Farm

G RANNY'S BARN WAS large and roomy and had stalls for the two horses, one mule, and two cows. There was a corncrib in the barn and a smoke house just outside the barnyard. The barnyard gate had a chain around its post, and when we went in and out of the barn lot we always fastened the gate. I learned that leaving it open courted fate. Once I did not pull the chain through and fasten it. Later I had to walk about four miles to bring the horses back after they ran and kicked up their heels with old Flossy, our dog, hot on their trail. That one lesson was all I needed, and I never left the gate open again.

Near the gate was a large watering trough made of mountain slate and mortar. Here the livestock quenched their thirst and I refreshed my face by splashing it with water that was diverted from the spring to the barn by a wooden V-shaped trough supported by small forked tree branches. This filled the drinking trough at the barn. The trough at the spring could be moved aside when the barn trough was full, and in this way the animals always had fresh water to drink. Once in a while we saw a duck floating lazily along the trough in the cool, clear water.

When we needed water in the cabin, Granny took two buckets that hung on the wall, and I carried a smaller one she found for me. I followed her down the path to a spring near our cabin where we filled our buckets. Then we emptied the water into a holding tank in the kitchen. We had rain barrels at each corner of the cabin to catch rainwater, which we used for washing clothes, taking baths, washing our hair, and many other things. When we had no rainwater, we used water from the spring for all our chores. Water was plentiful in the mountain springs, brooks, and creeks, and there were many small waterfalls that supplied a bountiful amount for our use.

PEARL K. MCCULLOUGH

CHAPTER 6

My First Spring In The Mountains

WITH THE ARRIVAL of spring came an important event: All the ducks in Granny's barnyard had to be plucked. How well I remember that time of year! First we fed the ducks corn by sprinkling it on the ground; then we caught them one at a time. Granny tucked the duck's head under her arm, turned it over on its back, and proceeded to pull the light feathers, called down, which nature had provided them for the long, cold winter months. Granny explained that this was a necessity and I tried to help her, but I couldn't bear to take the down from these squawking fowls when they fought so bravely to retain it.

But Granny had a unique way of explaining why this was necessary. She left one hen and one drake unplucked just to show me that when warm weather arrived, the down really wasn't needed or wanted. I watched the ducks that summer as they held out their wings, puffing and blowing from the heat, and I knew, as always, Granny was right! They really didn't need the down come warm weather, so the following spring I helped catch them and was even willing to hold them, while Granny pulled away at the under feathers. She showed me how nature takes care of this, too, because the ducks had already shed a lot of the warmest, lightest feathers once they were no longer needed.

Once while we were studying this aspect of nature, a thunderstorm put in a sudden appearance. Lightening struck the clothesline in our backyard, danced down the entire length of it and ended with a crash into the post. Granny had been showing me the bare breast and under-wings of the old drake that having lost his precious feathers, had squawked the whole time. With the flash of lightening, Granny jumped to her feet, threw the old drake high into the air, and cried out, "Lord have mercy!" Within seconds we were safe in the house, with my lesson on nature not soon to be forgotten.

One morning I walked outside to find that spring had put in a sudden appearance. The hills seemed to welcome the beautiful sunrise, and I stared, amazed at the changes that had taken place in the last few days.

Granny was looking over the vegetable garden, pulling a weed here and there, while I, a child, tried to take in the transformation that somehow brought excitement not only to me but also to all the wild creations in the mountains.

I heard so many sounds, and turned my head sideways in order to catch them more clearly. I heard the crow far off, the squirrel as he chattered in a tree nearby, and the old rooster as he held his head high and gave out a very strong crow. I think I even heard a bee as he flew by my face with a wee buzz and landed on a plant, seeking the sweet nectar that sustains life. I saw where a lizard had stretched out on a piece of wood as he sunned himself. I felt delight at all that nature was showing me, and I looked to Granny with a smile.

"Yes," said Granny, "spring has sprung, but the ground is too cold for planting so we must leave the young plants in the hotbeds another week or so. Don't be in such a hurry, my child."

We checked the hotbeds that Granny had started two weeks earlier. They were in the shed room in long wooden beds filled with rich soil from the nearby hills. I watched Granny as she worked, telling me in great detail step by step how this was accomplished. First, she washed the seeds in warm water and allowed them to stand in the water several hours. Then with a small wooden stick made especially for this purpose, she placed each seed in rows of soil just so deep. She covered the seeds with soil, then tacked a large piece of toe sack on top of the box. (Toe sack was another name for a burlap bag.)

PEARL K. MCCULLOUGH

Granny looked after these little seedlings as if they were children. She bathed them, put them to bed, covered them, and watched over them; soon they were on their own to grow and mature.

A day did not go by that I did not, with help, check on these plants. Nothing happened at first during the cold weather. Then, as it became somewhat warmer, I saw a few small cracks in the soil. I felt so excited when Granny told me the seeds were waking up.

The weather warmed a little more each day, and I was allowed to peek under the toe sack cover. Now the seeds had pushed themselves up two or three inches, almost touching the sack cover. We had been sprinkling a small amount of water on the beds. Now we removed the cover every day, and soon left the seed beds uncovered at night. In the early morning I often found myself passing Granny's bed on tiptoe so as not to awaken her, to check on the plants and also a branch that had a cocoon hanging from it that Granny had taken from a tree. We found two cocoons in the forest, but my curiosity had gotten the best of me; when I heard a scratching one night, I opened the enclosed pod and took the small creature out. He died within a few minutes. I did not tell Granny, I didn't need to, as she always knew. I began to think she had many eyes back and front. She just shook her head and told me not to open the other one.

The next time I heard the scratching I ran to let her know, and she took the branch inside the cabin and hung it over my bed, reminding me again not to open this one. The cocoon was pushed open one day when I went to check, as I just couldn't wait to see what would happen.

Oh, such a sight! The large moth was on the side table near my bed, pumping up his wings. I watched as he spread them up and down. They seemed to get larger each time, and more beautiful. The color was most vivid. Each wing had a large eye on it. Granny came in, and I received another lesson in nature. She told me the eyes were to frighten other insects away. She explained that pumping the wings strengthened the moth's lungs and body, but the main thing was to not free it from the cocoon, so that it could become strong before it emerged. Struggle was surely a necessity for them, and too much help could become disabling. We took the moth outside and put him on a low tree branch. According to Granny, he needed to rest for two hours. Later when I checked, he had flown away.

The days in the mountains with Granny were long and happy. We spent hours wandering the woods. Sometimes I helped dig in the rich, leaf-covered woods for the many different kinds of leaves, herbs, roots, and even berries that filled the shelves in Granny's pantry, so that when winter arrived, Granny had the cure for many mountain illnesses that struck the old and young alike. I spent many winter evenings helping her tend the sick and watching as she comforted a family when death took a loved one. Often she prepared the body for burial, and since I was with Granny, I found myself learning to do all these things and more. Granny never ceased to be amazed when she found me looking for the mountain remedies on my own. Soon I knew each one at a glance, and what they could be used for.

CHAPTER 7

Summertime

I SPENT MY first summer with Granny roaming the hillsides, making friends with as many wild creatures as I dared. Once I opened a trap to free a young fox. I was holding him by the nape of the neck, his head back, mouth forced open with my thumb and little finger in each corner of his mouth so he couldn't bite me. Just as I pushed my foot down to open the trap, my thumb slipped inside his mouth. The fox was freed, but I lost the knuckle of my right thumb in the process! Granny knew I was freeing the wild animals because I loved them. When she sewed my thumb up, she told me not to go near the traps again. However, I did free many more wild things the following winter, unless I knew they were to be used for meat.

The floor of the mountain forest was alive with a pulsating hum. One afternoon I spotted a bee tree on our walk and I hurried to let Granny know. On our way home we stopped by our neighbor's home and told him where the bee tree could be found. A few days later, Granny told me that Jeb had brought us a passel of honey from the wild bee tree and said he was saving us a hive as well as some bees when they swarm next year. Granny has gotten beehives before just this way. When she located the bees she would pass the location to one of our neighbors, who in return would give her honey and some bees as well. She had several beehives that had a special place near the garden. Granny was careful to leave them plenty of honey for the winter months, and often put some of our honey back into the hives if she found they needed it. Granny's honey was traded as well as seed corn and other commodities that were bartered back and forth.

Seed corn was always needed in the spring, so when Granny heard of a trader taking goods to the mountain market, she always loaded two or three large bags on his wagon. On his return trip later in the week, the trader brought with him whatever Granny had requested in exchange for her corn.

I remember we used a lot of salt for curing corn, beans, cabbage, meats, and even eggs for use in the winter season. The eggs were boiled, the shells removed, then put into large glass jars that held several dozen eggs. Salt and apple cider vinegar were added along with a small amount of sugar. The jars were not sealed, but rather left on the sideboard so everyone could help themselves. Granny also took her eggs in a food basket to mountain people in need, along with other foods she reserved for special needs. No one went hungry if my Granny knew about them! Caring about others, I quickly learned, was a specialty with the mountain people.

There were places in the hills we dared not enter, however, such as where the mountain stills were kept. Granny knew where most of them were. Men that made mountain whisky ran these. Granny always kept one gallon in our cabin. She used this in many of her medications. She used the word "curer" when explaining the reason to me. I watched as she mixed these herbs, leaves, roots, and whisky. Sometimes I held a small funnel while she filled small bottles, then carefully placed them on a shelf in the keeping room.

CHAPTER 8

Winter Months

GRANNY WELCOMED THE weather changes, but was forever telling me we must prepare for such-and-such weather. Winter was the most difficult season, and preparing for the winter months kept us as busy as bees.

Thanksgiving and Christmas were times of reflection, and I learned we must take time from our daily lives to do this. Granny started early making gifts for friends and neighbors for Christmas. She showed me how to hem baby diapers, what she called *hippens*, by hand, and between the two of us we made several dozen 'hippens' for families that had the pleasure of welcoming a wee one into their midst. We made these from white sacks that many of the mountain folk received their commodities in. Some were colored with print and some were solid white, while others were burlap bags. The white ones were boiled in lye soap water that bleached them, then were rinsed several times and dried on a line or a bush. Then we were ready for mending and sewing.

CHAPTER 9

Trading

WHEN WE HAD more than we needed for our own use, Granny traded these items for something else we did need. Items that Granny was famous for having, such as seed corn, dried peas and beans, lard and lye soap were popular trading items. I remember Granny saved old butter, grease drippings and any grease products not fit to eat to be made into lye soap. Chickens, ducks, guinea fowl and even crushed corncobs mixed with animal food for horses and mules were typical items used for trading. Corncobs in large baskets were found in every privy in the mountains and upper highlands, used as a substitute for toilet paper. No waste was tolerated in the mountain community.

Granny knew what plants could be eaten; many blossoms from plants were not only edible, they were very nourishing, as were wild onions known as "ramps". Wild gooseberries and fox grapes grew everywhere and were harvested, dried in the sun and stored for use in the winter season.

Another tradable item was face soap that Granny made from butter mixed with flower petals that had a pleasant aroma and a small amount of wood ash. This mixture was cooked slowly for hours in a wash pot on an open fire. I loved the smell and always associated it with the smell of clean laundry after being sun dried. All these items were harvested early in the fall. Any time there was a surplus, it was passed on to those in need. Our shed room was well-stocked with food items for cooking and many others were for medical purposes. I remember salt was one item we had to buy or trade for and was important for cooking as well as preserving and curing foods. Granny made sure she always had several sacks of salt on hand.

CHAPTER 10

Granny Was a Healer

WE DIDN'T HAVE time for idleness. There was always something to do, if not for ourselves, then for others. Granny taught me to do this with gladness and to always be thankful when I was made aware of the needs of others.

Granny was often called on to tend the sick and dying, to sew up cuts; she treated animals as well as humans. She was surely the wonder woman of those beautiful, majestic mountains.

I recall the day she sewed up a man who had been slashed with a hog-killing knife in a fight. I could barely look when the men brought him in a wagon to my Granny. He was bleeding so badly that the blood had run almost the length of his body. Granny instructed the men to cut off his shirt. She ran into the house and reappeared with a handful of soot from the back of the fireplace. She quickly rubbed this into the open cut and shouted, "Get me some spiderwebs from the barn." Those she placed on the open wound and held them there with both hands. The bleeding stopped very shortly. She then washed her hands in oil from the lamp, dropped a sack needle and coarse thread into the lamp oil to clean them, and then sewed the man up, afterwards saying with a smile, "Take him home now. I'll look in on him tomorrow." Seeing this helped me through hard times later in life.

Granny's Treatment for Worms

Worms in children was something that should not exist according to my dear granny. I remember how she fought to eradicate this in the mountain area where we lived. The symptoms of a child having worms were most often a swollen tummy and the child having to "go" all the time, perhaps eight or ten times a day. The mountain children were dewormed every spring using three drops of pine oil administered in a teaspoon of sugar, or molasses, or cane juice, the juice from cane before it is made into syrup or molasses. This was given several times if Granny detected worms in the stool of a child. However, the dose of medication was once a week. More than that could be dangerous.

Another known worm remedy was turpentine or lamp oil (this was used a hundred years ago) in a teaspoon of sugar or molasses syrup. I'd learned that many children died of worms in the mountain regions. Granny watched over me like a mother hen, and I too was given this concoction twice a year, but only one dose at a time. She recommended collecting and eating wild mountain greens as a good spring tonic.

Granny never found me infested with worms. She insisted on inspecting my stool as she collected it, trying not to embarrass me while doing so.

To get babies and very young children to take their medicine, *sugartits* were made by dipping cloth in wild cherry wine to which medicine was added and they sucked on this sweetness.

Granny told me children should swallow live minnows several times a year as a source of fish oil. We fished in the mountain streams for the tiny silver fish (no longer than one or two inches), setting fish traps made of wire in the shape of a large cone. We used chicken innards as bait in the traps. When the fish went in they could not get out. We had them often and caught enough to share with others. I had a difficult time at first swallowing this small creature, but later I did not mind at all.

During the second year I stayed with Granny, a rash of whooping cough hit the mountain region and soon it reached epidemic proportions. We were up night and day helping these people. Granny had made a syrup of leaves for the cough. First the leaves were cooked on the wood stove and squashed into a pulp in a large wooden bowl used when we made bread. Then Granny let me help her finish it. How well I remember watching as the mixture began to thicken. It looked as smooth as honey. Whiskey, honey, and rock candy were added just before the cough medicine was poured into a large crock jar Granny kept for this purpose. This mixture was given to those suffering from whooping cough. Not one ounce of this precious liquid was wasted, as there was always need in the mountains.

Granny carefully measured out this syrup in ounces into small bottles, and each family received only as much as was needed. Then, after Granny gave the elders instructions regarding taking the medicine, we were off again. On and on, deep into the mountains we walked, leaving our cabin door unlocked, as was the custom of mountain people. Our livestock was taken care of by Granny's daughter, Fern, until we returned, perhaps a week later.

Far into the mountains we went. Our steps were as soft as our featherbeds at home. My mind was like a dry riverbed, nothing moving. Everything was standing perfectly still, no sounds to be heard as we walked on the spongy trail winding in and out among the trees and large mountain ferns that covered miles upon miles of the mountaintop.

PEARL K. MCCULLOUGH

Granny stopped to change the sacks on our horses' backs, as they had slipped to the side and would likely fall off. These sacks were filled with precious medicines we gathered for those ill with whooping cough. My legs hurt, and we stopped to rest for a short time. The air was so pure and fresh, and Granny reminded me to breathe deeply as we climbed higher into the mountains.

As we came into view of a wee cabin, a dog greeted us. Granny allowed him to smell her hands and gave him a few gentle pats on his head. There were two children here. I stayed in the yard while inside she made tea with herbs and leaves for the children. Then Granny took rock candy from the horses' backpacks and mixed it with whiskey and the dark tea she had just brewed. She took leave after telling the mother how much to give each child, and instructed her not to overuse it.

After a week or so visiting the mountain people and caring for the ill, we returned home to Granny's cabin.

CHAPTER 11

My Silence is Breached

LITTLE DID I know that the whooping cough would tear down my wall of protection and silence and leave me defenseless. I caught the whooping cough even with the vile-smelling asphidity bag Granny made me wear around my neck, which was to have prevented me from contracting any infectious germs that attacked the mouth, throat and bronchial tubes. I started coughing, and on the third day my fever was so high that Granny would not leave me, even to attend the mountain people she loved so dearly.

I coughed so much I lost my breath. I was very much afraid, but knowing Granny was there with me was most reassuring. I felt her loving hands on my burning brow, pushing my hair back from my face. I found myself drifting off to sleep, waking and seeing Granny there beside me, and drifting off again and again.

I remember smelling the whiskey-rock candy and tea that had helped so many others, felt the hot mixture as it was forced into my mouth time after time with a spoon. I wept silent tears as Granny prepared mustard and wild onion poultices for my chest. For a while I was aware of what was going on, then for a few days I knew nothing. I was very ill, my grandmother told me much later.

I awakened one day to find myself wrapped in a heavy woolen blanket, with mustard and onion poultices on my back and chest. I knew without being told that I had pneumonia, since this was one of Granny's mountain remedies that had pulled many of the people of the hills back from the jaws of death.

Finally, wrapped in a blanket, I was allowed to sit in a chair covered with a warm sheepskin. My feet rested on a flat rock that had been heated in the fireplace, then wrapped in cloth.

Granny barely talked for many days after I began my recovery and could sit out on the front porch in the big rocker. When she finally did talk, she started to tell me about her life when she was a young girl. Then she asked me if I wanted to tell her why I was so unhappy. I could only shake my head. She took my face in her hands and made me look straight into her eyes. "You were delirious, Katherine; for days on end I listened to your mad ravings, and I have been trying to sort out and untangle your thoughts. Child, why haven't you told Granny what happened to you? In your delirium, you begged your father not to hurt you. Now tell me all about it. Perhaps it will ease the pain of remembering."

I believe in my fevered ramblings I must have confused my father with Mr. Roberts, or that Granny misunderstood my mumbling. I continued shaking my head. I couldn't bring myself to speak of it.

"Please don't pretend you can't talk because I know now that you can. Why haven't you told Granny, dear child, what happened to you? You see, Katherine, I know your father raped you."

I could only shake my head at first, but then found myself screaming. My voice grew louder and louder, the first sounds I had made in almost two years, since the doctor tried to examine me. Tears streamed down my face, and I held onto Granny with all my might. She allowed me to cry until I could cry no more.

Granny went to her own sleep of death believing my father had raped me. I tried later to tell her otherwise but she never believed I wasn't trying to protect him, although she knew how much I disliked him. She was sure I needed to reassure myself my father wasn't to blame for what had happened to me.

Once I started talking again, Granny and I had long talks in front of the open fire. I finally felt loved and wanted, so I shared my thoughts with her. How wonderful to feel that you can be close to someone you love and be able to put your trust in that person! I told her about freeing wild things from the traps and of putting human scent (taken from the privy) on the trails so the animals would change their routes. I told her too of watching bees swarm, and how I had picked up the queen and put her into the hive and watched with pleasure when all the other bees followed her in. Granny knew of this; she had shown me the queen bee and had told me she was the largest bee in the hive, so I knew just what to look for.

I gathered eggs and sang at the top of my voice, and the mountains echoed back the sound of many voices. To find a new plant or vine I could identify from Granny's description filled me with pleasure.

One by one I learned the secrets that nature hid in the mountains. I made soap of the best quality, and knew just what leaves to use for fragrance. Granny taught me to quilt, make pickles, relishes, and canned foods that could be eaten during the winter months. She showed me how to dry food that could be stored and used when food wasn't too plentiful. This was food that could be kept for years without spoiling, as long as it was kept dry and free from any kind of moisture. I was taught to prepare mountain food in such a way that it would melt in one's mouth. Our pantry overflowed with canned foods of every description, kept in Mason jars, a few of which blew their tops from spoilage.

CHAPTER 12

Aunt Hat

SOMETIMES WE SPENT Sundays with one of Granny's friends, Aunt Hat. I never knew her real name. Granny told me once Aunt Hat was ill with a very high fever. During that time she lost all her hair, and it never grew back. Afterwards, one never saw Aunt Hat without a large black hat covering her head, hence, her name.

Whenever we visited, Aunt Hat always had a beautiful meal prepared, white tablecloth and all. She also had a teapot, and always allowed me to pour the tea. Often she tied the tealeaves in a cloth bag, and we used it several times. Tea was not common in the mountains and few people had it. If you could afford to purchase tea, as often as it was ordered, the mailman delivered it to your mailbox, which might be some four or five miles away.

Aunt Hat had what the mountain people called "the mother of bread". This was kept in a large crock in the springhouse. She would give her lady friends a hunk of this dough and tell them not to allow it to die, but to keep adding a little flour and water (whole wheat was best, she said), and remember to feed it often. Later I learned cooks also refer this to as a "starter". Granny said "bread mother" goes back hundreds of years and can be passed around for generations. The beginning process is referred to as a sponge.

As I recovered from the whooping cough, Aunt Hat stated flatly that the two of them would fatten me up, and this they started to do immediately with loads of help from Granny's mountain medicine and tonics they gave me frequently. I took it all and basked in the sunshine of their love. Aunt Hat's stories often caused me to cry when they were sad, and when she told the happy ones, I was happy and showed it. The funny ones often left me lying on the floor holding my sides, hugging one of Aunt Hat's corn shuck brooms, and pretending I was one of the mountain people she was spinning a yarn about.

One day Aunt Hat appeared at Granny's cabin and stated emphatically, "I'm here to do some sewing for you and your grandmother." She started unloading things from a large basket—ribbons, ruffles, and lace—she had made herself. When she got to the bottom of her basket she pulled four pieces of yard goods out and held them up to me. "These will do nicely," she said with a smile. "I hear you are going to an all-day meeting and dinner on the ground on Sunday. Let's cut and sew today for you, and tomorrow will be Granny's day." And so it was.

The table was cleared "a-for-hand" as Granny would say, meaning the table was cleared first; then the cloth was spread out nice and flat. I stood as Aunt Hat measured me with her hands while talking to herself: "Three hands here, four hands there, one and a half hands around the neck." Often she wrote something on her hand. I wondered how this could ever work. Soon she set to the cutting, and piece by piece she put this amazing creation together into a dress. I was almost afraid to look. When she stopped for a bite to eat, she covered everything up with a sheet from the big box at the foot of Granny's bed.

When Aunt Hat was finished, I loved my dress. She had dyed the cloth before making the dress, and it was as blue as clear midday sky. It had a small lace collar to grace my neck, lace the color of the cream from our springhouse. The sleeves were puffed, the length was long, hanging about four inches below my knees. I questioned this and was told I would grow taller, and the dress would fit me for a long time. When I tried the dress on, I did not want to take it off. Aunt Hat insisted, though, so after about an hour I removed the dress and put all the pieces of leftover material in Granny's quilting box.

Granny didn't say one word when she discovered the following morning that I'd taken the dress to bed with me that night. She just smiled. I was pleased when she allowed me to place my new dress on the bed during the day.

Granny's dress was light brown with long sleeves and a high neck with a collar that covered much of her neck. The Indian lady Aunt Hat knew had dyed the material. I was told that deer urine had been used to dye Granny's dress, along with some added hickory bark.

Granny had told me the big chest at the foot of her bed was her very first chest. When she married, her uncle built this piece of household furniture for her. He hand carved the floral pattern with a handheld wood chisel, and polished it with beeswax. Its beauty was outstanding. I loved to run my hands over the wood and had to have Granny help me lift the heavy lid and take a few minutes to examine the contents. Within the chest were many treasures: pieces of cloth, lace, pictures, long pieces of hair tied with ribbon, several pieces of broken dishes, and last but not least, a long baby's dress made from thin material with lots of needlework. When Granny unfolded the dress, a hatpin fell to the floor. This had been placed between the folds of the dress. I picked the hatpin up and handed it to Granny, and saw that tears had fallen from her eyes onto the dress. She blotted the tears with her apron, replaced the items, and walked out to drink from the gourd dipper that hung from the wall outside.

Aunt Hat said we don't feel or see half the things in life we are meant to feel and see. She told me one day that we only use a small amount of our senses. I couldn't understand what she meant. Granny, who had the answer to everything, or so I thought, said when asked, "That's Hati-talk. Don't ask me, she's the book reader."

Granny sent me often to Aunt Hat's cottage to learn to read, and I began reading to Granny each night by our oil lamp. She sat as still as a mouse, never saying a word. We lingered as she rocked in the rocking chair near the fire, not wanting to retire for the night. It was times like that when the world seemed so far away, and we in turn felt no part of it. Our own world was there, safe as the eagle's nest high in a tree, with sturdy branches lined with feathers to make a haven on earth for the young eaglets until they spread their wings.

In addition to reading, I sought Aunt Hat's advice on addition, subtraction, and many other things. She was a kind, loving person that had a great effect on my life in the years to come. Aunt Hat encouraged me to write short stories as I saw them, about the mountain people, my love for animals, and most of all about Granny, the person that constructed my own eagle's nest that had supported me and protected me when evil winds battered my almost lifeless form. Granny had instilled in me the knowledge that being beaten down but rising up again, tall and strong, is something one can do.

One such evening, Aunt Hat's cabin was put to rest. The door was locked and the shutters in our bedroom were opened. The fire was out and had been for some time. The lampshades had been cleaned and set aside for the next night. Only one lamp had a shade. This one sat next to Aunt Hat's bed with matches, should she need to light the lamp during the night.

We undressed in the darkness. Aunt Hat had given me a long gown that I pulled up as I walked to the trundle bed that had been prepared for me.

In the moonlight that flooded our bedroom, I tried not to watch as Aunt Hat took her hat off and hung it on a rack attached to the wall. She quickly went to a small bedside table, took a cap from a drawer, and put it on her head. I knew from my experience with Granny that women sometimes slept in a cap made from material left over from their gown for sleeping. As I snuggled down in the covers for sleep, I heard Aunt Hat's faint sigh. A night bird called nearby, and I drifted into a world of dreams, but I was awakened hours later screaming as I flung myself about on the bed. Aunt Hat's gentle hands reached out to embrace and comfort me. In despair, I cried for several minutes before I was awake enough to understand that nothing bad was happening to me. I was there with Aunt Hat in her cabin, and everything was all right.

In vain we tried to sleep again, but finally we got out of bed and started a small fire in the fireplace. Here we sat and talked. I wasn't asked any questions regarding my dream. Aunt Hat was calm and went about making us hot cider. She hugged me as she put the cup into my shaking hands. Then she took a book from a nearby table and opened it, and began to read. I closed my eyes and listened to the musical sound of her beautiful voice. She was reading of the history of Boston. When I opened my eyes, I saw that she had tears rolling running down her cheeks. I put my cup down and went to hug and comfort her, as she had so recently comforted me, and I wondered about Aunt Hat's dreams. Were they hurtful as mine were?

On our way home the next day Granny wanted to hear about all that had happened since our parting the night before. I told Granny that Aunt Hat had cried last night when she was reading to me about Boston. I wanted to know why, but Granny just shook her head and said, "Well, some things are better left unsaid." I knew this was not the time to question Granny's judgment regarding Aunt Hat crying and we would talk when the time was right—or rather, Granny would talk, and I would listen as befitted a young girl at that time and place.

On the way to our cabin we stopped to pick up our new milk cow Granny had left at our neighbor's for breeding. Granny called this "servicing," but didn't go into any details that might have explained this further. The cow was put on a lead line and we walked together on the path, the cow not far behind. The large bull enclosed in a pen watched us as we closed the main gate to the barn and Granny spoke to the owner. Perhaps they were bartering for the service fee. The calf would arrive in early spring. The bull was a Jersey, the same breed as our cow. Granny said they were the best milk cows.

We arrived home to find someone had been there and left two sacks of salt on our porch, a jug of corn whiskey for Granny's medicine, and a small hooked rug made from strips of homespun material left over from clothes sewn by one of the many women who exchanged material and clothing for other goods. Granny seemed to know who had been there, what each person left, and the things they would need in exchange. Bartering was a way of life to these mountain people.

CHAPTER 13

Mountain Indian Lore

M OST OF THE Indians in our area lived on the reservation at Cherokee, North Carolina. However, we often saw one couple in particular with whom we would talk. They came to Granny's cabin on several occasions to spend time talking about mountain medicine and cures that Granny used daily.

I remember hearing them discussing a cold river dip if one has a high fever. Granny told them this was not right and should not be used especially in the winter season, because this could cause pneumonia and possibly death. The Indian laughed and said he had used this many times and few had died. Granny explained she always wrapped sick people in blankets to keep them warm, giving them hot whiskey with honey, and washing their body in cool water until the fever broke.

I sat in on many talks of mountain medication, cures, and stories of overuse of the nightshades. Granny told me what she called nightshades were things that had bare roots that never saw the sun. These were to be used only in small amounts and in certain times not at all. Forest nightshades are never to be eaten, as they can cause death. One must know them and the effects they may cause, and be well aware of their potent effect when used.

The Indians that visited Granny's cabin were kind and gentle, and Granny told me they were most careful of life in the forest. They killed only when they needed meat and never allowed the animals to suffer lingering deaths. She told me the Indians tracked a wounded deer for miles to be sure it did not suffer unnecessarily. This was the way by which they lived, claiming close relationship with all God's creatures from the smallest squirrel to the large bear or wolf, which could be seen often in the thick mountain range. "These people," Granny said to me, "are the heart and soul of the Great Smoky Mountain Range." Then she added, "We are the outsiders, man trying to change the ways of the Indians. We must accept them and respect them the way they are. One does not need to agree with someone else's lifestyle in order to show love and kindness."

The Indians believed the red-tailed hawk was a good omen. To see one near your home was rewarding, but to have one make a nest to raise their young near you was a special event and brought many good things to one's family and life.

CHAPTER 14

Ringing the Bell

I OPENED MY eyes to a new day, threw back the feather bed, and looked out the window Granny had opened wide. This was her message to me, "Time to rise and shine." I slipped my feet into slippers Granny had knitted for me when I first arrived. When I walked into the kitchen, its warmth enfolded me and I felt good about being there with Granny. I smelled apples cooking, and a pot of dried beans called "leather britches" were singing a merry song as they bubbled away in a large pot with long legs in the large fireplace that we often used for cooking.

Granny gave me a big hug and handed me a copper cup of hot apple cider to drink. I sat by the fire and drank it slowly. Later I had a bowl of corn meal mush with wild honey and cream that I'd learned to like with dear Granny's encouragement.

I saw on the sideboard that five apple pies were cooling, and Granny had her large basket sitting nearby, ready for four of the pies, which we'd take to other elderly mountain people, some living five or six miles away. Sometimes we used the buggy, but often we walked if the trails were treacherous. The supplies we had on hand were shared with others, and a bit of bartering took place. The medicines Granny gleaned from gathering herbs, leaves, and bark from trees in the hills and valleys of North Carolina were taken along. She selected certain roots from plants only she knew should be taken.

*   *   *

"It's time to ring the bell now."

I heard those words several times while living with Granny. Most families have a large bell on a pole perhaps fifteen feet in the air, and this bell can be heard for miles. The mountain people know something has happened when a neighbor's bell rings, and will gather as soon as possible. Most of the time a bell is rung due to an accident or death, and sometimes a fire.

I remember such an occasion when Granny pulled me out of bed in the dead of night. "Make haste, child," she stated. "There's a fire, I can see the light from the porch, and it's not five miles away." When we got outside, I could hear the bell ringing. She turned to me, took me by the hand, and we hurried off. Granny put a finger in her mouth and then held her hand as high in the air as she could reach to gauge from which direction the wind was blowing.

When we arrived, the house was almost consumed by flames. Many people were talking and rushing about trying to be of help. Before we returned to our own place Granny gathered three of the children in hand, and they stayed with us for a week. The three slept in my bed, and I slept on the floor. I remember I was upset when I discovered the five-year-old boy had wet my shuck mattress. Granny shamed me, scolding me severely for complaining. She made me another mattress because I refused to sleep on the old one.

The very next day, I saw wagons go by our place with lumber, and many men walking, some carrying tools. Granny explained that they were beginning work on a new cabin for the family that had lost their home. The following days were busy, and filled with love for the mountain people. Granny took me with her each day and we went out in our buggy, gathering all sorts of things for this family—canned goods in mason jars, clothes, bedding, dishes, a clothesline, pots and pans—everything one would need for a family of eight. One little lady gave us a chamber pot, and I thought to myself, *I know a five-year-old boy that could sure use that pot!*

The third day when we went by we saw that the cabin was well on its way, a good thing because our shed room was bursting with the many gifts that had been given so far, and much more was to come. I know now that most of those people did without themselves in order to help their neighbor, and they were happy to do so.

At the end of a long day, my bed was warm and cozy. I pulled the covers to my chin and turned on my side, hearing the shuck mattress make that rustling sound I'd grown accustomed to. I relaxed and looked out the shuttered window that Granny left open in the early part of the night.

The night creatures were out, and I listened to the sounds surrounding the cabin. Night birds were nearby in the trees and I heard them clearly. The fox barked for his mate. A wild pig, or perhaps a domestic one, foraged in the forest hoping to turn up a meal. The ole' owl was in good voice as he hooted away, then swooped down, the wind making a whooshing sound as he caught a fleeing barn mouse. Some nights I lay awake for hours on end to enjoy this evening serenade. There were always plenty of questions for Granny on the morrow, and as usual, she had answers to most if not all of them. Finally I drifted off to sleep and dreamed of the moon and the light that seemed to awaken and bring to life the hidden joys of nightlife in the forest.

CHAPTER 15

Laying Out the Dead

THE SUN SLOWLY vanished, sending beams of light into the mountain forest. They highlighted the leaves and bushes, turning the forest into a glimmering gold for a few seconds before we were enclosed in darkness. We were on our way to visit a neighbor who was ill. A young girl had come for Granny, and now we walked in single file after Granny, stopping once for her to light a small lantern.

Shortly we arrived at the top of a high cliff and Granny stopped "The cabin is just below," she said. "You can see the faint light from a lamp near the window." We caught our breath and then proceeded down the mountain carefully, holding hands. Fireflies were everywhere, and they were so beautiful. As we opened the garden gate, the sweet smell of honeysuckle and other plants filled our lungs and we paused to savor the mountain aromas I had learned to love.

A large dog came out to meet us, and Granny allowed him to smell her hand and she stooped to pet him.

We walked into a clean cabin furnished, as usual, with furniture made by hand by one of the mountain people, perhaps by the very man who was now ill.

A large safe (a cabinet with doors covered with screen or wire to keep rats and mice away) stood in the corner of the room. A table with benches had a glass jar with a spoon in it at each place. In minutes Granny had the family's six children sitting at the table, and she cut cornbread for everyone. After eating the cornbread and milk, the six young ones were put on pallets on the floor in the safekeeping room for the night.

I looked with eyes of wonder at a full moon through the screen wire that covered the one window in the keeping room. The room had many different smells of food of every description, food grown in the mountains and stored here, including herbs, and often shucks and feathers for the mattresses. There were several bags of assorted seeds that were saved and considered precious, in case of any type of drought or disaster that might affect the harvest of new seed for planting. This was a necessity for survival in every household.

The next morning after washing our faces and hands, we had the usual cornmeal mush with honey and milk. Much later we picked apples from a nearby tree and ate them. I remember one young boy climbed the tree and offered me a large green apple that was not ready to pick. His sister warned me this could cause a stomachache. I was quick to leave the apple uneaten.

Most of that day was spent outside the cabin. In late afternoon the mother came out, gathered her children around her, and told them their father had died. Granny came out to take me in hand, telling me she was going to be busy laying the man out. As usual, I was full of questions and waited impatiently for answers, and Granny shut me up by saying, "I will talk about it later." I have to wait for Granny's time for talking about these things.

I watched as she returned to the cabin, and I sank into the tall grass nearby and looked up into a blue sky, seeing white puffs of clouds float by as I lay on my back chewing a blade of grass I plucked from the rich soil. I remember thinking, "What in the world is 'laying out'?" I knew I'd find out soon, as Granny did not believe in leaving anything unfinished or any question unanswered.

The funeral was the next day. The bell rang out and people came who lived miles away, and the table was laden with food as soon as the men removed it from the kitchen to the yard. Everyone arrived with baskets of food.

The father was laid to rest just before noon. The reader of scripture was a tall, bearded man who walked with a long walking stick. He spoke differently from the mountain people. I now think he was Scottish.

Later Granny accepted his kind offer to take us home in his buggy, and we arrived back at our cabin before dark. Our animals had been taken care of in our absence by other neighbors as usual. Granny made soup for supper, along with cornbread made some time ago.

Our eyes were heavy with sleep, and our bones tired and weary, so off to bed. Sleep came quickly as we both drifted off after saying goodnight to each other. No looking out the window that night, and no dreams. We rested blissfully as the mountain mist enfolded us for the night.

Another Layout-Out

I recall a particular day when a man had died and we went to help with the laying out. Granny had me sit on the porch while she and another lady bathed, dressed and prepared this man on the kitchen table before he was placed in his coffin. Men were in the yard, building the pine coffin to be used for the man's burial. A custom among the mountain people was to save lumber from the first pine tree cut on their land. They keep this lumber to be used as a coffin for the man of the house.

After preparing the body, Granny and the other lady came outside where the men were working at planing the wood and rubbing it down with a large sheepskin that had been soaked in bear grease and lamp oil.

The bell outside was rung so their mountain neighbors knew the time had come for the burial service.

PEARL K. MCCULLOUGH

CHAPTER 16

Harvest Time

G RANNY OPENED THE door, and I, close behind her, felt a change in the cool mountain air. It was crisp, and the leaves on the trees near our cabin had started to change color. I shielded my eyes with my hand as dancing sunbeams filled our cabin and the small yard outside with the light of midmorning. Granny took the dipper hanging from a peg on the wall of our porch, dipped it into the bucket of water, and drank slowly. Filling the gourd dipper again, she handed it to me and I quenched my thirst.

I knew when Granny was ready she would lay out our plans for the day. She always included me, making me feel important. She often asked, "Do you think today would be a good day to dig the potatoes, take up the cabbage, or shell the corn for hominy?"

I might say, "We could wait, it's early in the fall season to dig potatoes." Then she reminded me emphatically, "Time waits for no man." In no time we were busy working, and Granny, as usual, had a lesson for the day. When I started digging the ground up, cutting into the potatoes, she took the hoe from me and showed me how to work slowly and carefully in order not to cut the potatoes, then said, "Haste makes waste, child. A job worth doing is a job worth doing well."

We dug the potatoes and left them on the ground to dry for a few days before preparing them for winter storage. We pulled the cabbage heads up, leaving the root attached. Later we put them in the shed, placed in a large mound of pine needles and stored under a bank of soil. During the winter we just removed them as we needed them. We also dried and stored other fruits and vegetables for the winter–apples, carrots, onions, wild grapes, peaches, and crab apples.

At day's end we watched the sun set and enjoyed our twilight time together. As darkness fell we went inside, lighted the two lamps, and enclosed ourselves in the cabin for the night. We ate our supper of turnip greens cooked in a large three-legged iron pot that sat in the hot coals or could be hung from a rack in the fireplace. A piece of hog meat and corn dumplings added flavor and taste to this nourishing meal. We talked of our work and discussed our plans for the next day.

The remainder of the evening was ours to enjoy. Granny made this special time of the day so easy for me. She told me stories of long ago and sang songs she learned as a child. She sang as she rubbed my back or washed my feet or brushed my hair. At those times I saw a faraway look in her eyes and I knew her thoughts were miles away in another time.

At bedtime, Granny banked the fire for the night with several large logs, pulled the hooked rug she made back from the fireplace for safety, and the chamber pot was set between our beds. Flat rocks that had been heating near the fireplace were wrapped in a cloth and put under the covers at the foot of each bed to warm our feet. She tucked me into bed with the cornhusk mattress making comforting rustling sounds. As I snuggled down warm, tired, well-fed, and very sleepy, I heard Granny call out, "Don't forget to say your prayers. We must be thankful for the day."

I drifted off to sleep feeling so secure.

CHAPTER 17

Fall

FALL OF THE year in the mountains meant one thing for sure: apple butter-making time! People came from miles around to help peel and core apples. Then the large copper pots were taken out of the shed room where they had been stored the season before. Each pot held about twenty gallons. Granny started the apples to cooking in a small amount of water, and when the apples had cooked into pieces, she added sugar and spices.

That was an all day job, from sunup to sundown. The stirring went on constantly, using a large apple butter paddle that had holes in it so it moved more easily through the thick, heavy apple butter. It turned dark brown in color when it was ready to put into the jars, and the taste was equal to any dish served to a queen!

The three pots held sixty gallons. Sometimes we worked a full week making the apple butter, sixty gallons per day for five or six days. Granny never kept over forty gallons for our own use; the balance she traded to the mountain people for molasses, dried beans, herbs, roots, whiskey, seed corn, cordwood, and even a few days' work. These people really practiced the barter system!

The only thing I knew Granny to sell for money were eggs. To be sure they could not be resold as setting eggs, she stuck a pinhole in each egg to be sure it didn't hatch. She would give any friend or neighbor a setting of fifteen, but to sell them to a storekeeper and have him charge double for setting eggs wasn't to Granny's liking. She always told the storekeeper her eggs weren't for setting. The storekeeper told his customers that Granny didn't keep roosters—I guess he had tried to hatch her eggs! The people kept Granny's secret and probably laughed up their sleeves, as many of them had Granny's special breed of yellow buffs scratching about on the hillside.

Hog-killing time also came with the bareness of the trees, when one was sure the meat was safe from spoilage due to warm weather. We got up long before dawn, and had all the fires outside going and the pots boiling by the time the help arrived. Granny killed two or three hogs every year, and all at the same time. The hogs were shot in the pens and then a knife was used to stick them, so they would bleed properly. This was necessary, according to the mountain people, to keep the meat from spoiling. Then the boiling water was put into a wooden barrel that had been half-tilted in a dug out place in the ground. Two shovels-full of wood ash went into the barrel, and then the hog was placed in the hot water until the hair slipped off easily when pulled.

When the hair pulled easily, it was time to take the hog out and place the reverse end in the barrel. Then the scraping began. I've seen a hog dressed, hung, and ready to be gutted in thirty minutes from the time it was shot—if there was a good scald. If not, the hair would "set" on the hog if the water was too hot or too cold; if that happened, the entire day was spent shaving the hog, while he lay there with a look on his face that caused this saying, "As independent as a dead pig in the sunshine."

It took days to work up all the meat and start the sugar curing process for the joints. The intestines were scraped and used to stuff sausage. The fat was rendered out for lard in the large iron wash pots. The heart, lungs, part of the head, ears, and smelt were used to make sauce meat, which is known to many people as headcheese. Liver pudding was made from the liver and feet of a pig, with enough bone marrow to make it gel when cold. Often we made pickled pigs' feet, and if we had lots of cracklin', we ground them and stored them in a large earthen crock for making cracklin' cornbread. Not one pound of those hogs was wasted. Even the chitlins were prepared in such a way that one could eat well and enjoy it. The stomach was stuffed with cooked sweet potatoes and boiled in a large pot until done. The sausages were hung on poles in the smokehouse, and Granny and I took turns keeping a slow hickory bark fire going for fourteen days to cure them.

When we awoke one morning, the chickens were still on their roost. All the animals in our barn were tucked into their stalls and appeared to be warm and content to be there. The inside of the barn, I found, was warm and cozy. Granny told me there was heat in stable manure, and animals liked being close in the barn and stables in cold winter weather. The hogs and young shoats were making funny little *oink-oink* noises when we went to feed them. After eating, they returned to sleep in their beds of hay.

The milking cow was turned in with her calf after Granny milked her. This calf was a female, a purebred simple, much like the beloved mountain people. Granny planned to keep her. I was allowed to name her and gave her the name Daisy. Half the milk from Daisy's mother was left for Daisy. Granny wanted her to grow strong and healthy, as she would be a milking cow. This milk was not only for our use, but also the hogs and pigs frequently had milk in their trough. Occasionally Granny got an orphan calf from someone in the mountains when the family couldn't raise it. We would hold the mama cow while the strange calf nursed and would return the calf to its owner once it had grown a bit.

Sometimes we baked sweet potatoes and had them at noon with a cold glass of buttermilk from the springhouse. I loved watching the golden specks of butter floating on the fresh churned milk. I took the brown skin from the potatoes while they were still warm from the oven, or I'd take a whole potato into the woods, tossing it from hand to hand because it was hot or wrapping it in a large leaf, then eat it while sitting on the creek bank daydreaming, with my feet in the cold mountain stream. Then Granny would find me and cart me back to the house to eat at the table like so-called civilized people. Old Flossy, our dog, and I had several picnics, but Granny really believed in one eating at the table, so most of our eating-out episodes went on without Granny's consent, though we did have the ants' approval.

Sometimes at night, I opened the shutter in our bedroom and breathed deeply as Granny instructed. Many nights I saw the wild geese flying over our cabin and watched them with delight as the moon glistened on their lovely backs and necks. I could hear their honking until they were out of sight. I always said a silent prayer for their safe return in the spring. How I loved those geese! I'd watched them mate, seen them nesting, and waited impatiently for the little goslings to hatch. Granny taught me never to put my hand near a nest, but I've seen them as little balls of fluff rolling along the ground, heading for the stream.

Christmas and New Year

That year Christmas was cold and clear, and snow covered the ground. Our Christmas tree was dressed with popcorn on long strings, strung days ahead of this special day. Granny helped me string the popcorn with a large sack needle and thread (sometimes called twine by the mountain people). We also wrapped colorful cloth around hickory nuts, tied them with thread, and hung these on limbs and branches. A large crocheted star topped the tree, and flour and water made a paste that clung to the branches, giving a faint hint of snow. The tree stood in a water container until New Year's Day, and then we replanted this small, beautiful creation in the forest, and our decorations were put away for the following year. The white paste was washed off before we replanted the tree. Granny often went to show me the growing tree; I loved seeing the new growth.

We did not buy gifts but rather exchanged homemade things that were necessary in our day-to-day existence. But oh! The precious love and devotion was apparent, and given without hesitation.

Our typical Christmas dinner was ham or chicken, and once we had a wild turkey that a neighbor gave us. We were never in want of food, but it was plain.

New Year's Day we had black-eyed peas cooked with hog jowls and collard greens. Granny also cooked a pan of cracklin' cornbread, and we had cakes, pies, jelly, jams, and preserves. This was a New Year's mountain tradition, just as turkey on Thanksgiving is to most Americans. We never sat down to eat without first giving thanks, and I can never remember setting only two plates, though only the two of us ate. Granny insisted on having a third plate just in case someone came by who was hungry. If someone came by she didn't know well, a plate was fixed and carried to the back porch.

Granny never cracked nuts for cakes. When she was ready to bake a cake with nuts in it, she took her rifle and off we went into the woods to find a nut tree, or often a grove of them. We sat very still until the squirrels had eaten their fill, and then Granny shot a squirrel, skinned it, and emptied its stomach of nuts already ground! We washed the nuts in a thin cloth bag at the edge of a mountain stream, then off to the springhouse with the squirrel meat for dinner and nuts for our cake!

CHAPTER 18

Springtime—The Eagle's Nest

I RECALL ONE Sunday when Granny took me to the high meadows to see the eagle that had built a nest high in a majestic tree near a cliff that jetted out over the edge of a waterfall. High Meadow was a level, grassy plateau high up in the mountains. We wouldn't be able to see much of the nest, but we would see the eagle; perhaps her eggs had hatched. If so, we could watch her feed her chicks. One must be quiet and sit patiently as she hunted and returned frequently with food for the growing chicks.

Eagles are great hunters. You see them dart down from a high lookout to grab a mouse or other food, then hold them in their talons as they fly. Few are dropped.

My first trip to the eagle's nest was an exciting adventure. I was mesmerized at the wingspan of this magnificent creature as with little or no effort, she glided up and down on the cool mountain air currents. The freedom with which she moved was a sight for a young girl's eyes. My heart beat much faster as I leaned forward, watching every move the great bird made. All too soon Granny announced, "Time to go home." We'd been there three or four hours, but time had seemed to stand still, and I felt only thirty minutes or so had passed!

I had been with Granny about three and a half years. She had not, in all this time, abused me or been cross in any manner. She prayed upon arising in the morning before she dressed for the day, and at night before retiring, but I've heard her give someone a good dressing down and often send forth a few well-chosen cuss words, though each time followed by saying, "Excuse me, Lord."

She taught me the songs she knew as a girl, and the stories she told thrilled my heart and made me want so much to capture the days of long ago. She spoke of my mother, her beauty and her quiet mountain charm; how my father did not know even the meaning of love and had taken her away to be the mother of nine children in as many years; how she faced death many miles from her family with no one to care for her during the years of illness that resulted in her departure from this earth.

Granny worked hard, and she trained me just as my father had to never waste time. "Time is more precious than diamonds," she would say. "Never put off until tomorrow what you can do today."

CHAPTER 19

A Deformed Child

I RECALL ONE time when Granny took me with her when she went to deliver a baby. She left me in the yard to sit in a swing for several hours and frequently came to the door of the cabin and called to me, "Stay close by, child." I was obedient and did just as she instructed. I heard sounds indicating someone was in pain and voices that reached into the yard saying things I did not understand. I sat silently, a young girl in a strange world, seeking each day to peep behind the veil that shielded the mountain people from the outside world.

As we walked back to Granny's cabin, she told me we were going by Aunt Hat's, and I walked much faster. My love for Aunt Hat compared to a half-filled cup waiting to be filled to the brim. At first, Granny sat quietly with a cup of tea, and when she began to speak, tears filled her eyes and she was unable to stop the flow. Aunt Hat pulled her chair close to Granny's, took Granny's hand, and tried to comfort her. Finally, still crying, she told Aunt Hat about the baby she had delivered earlier that day.

"Now, Alice, you know that marriage to close kin can cause these things, no one has been able to change this. Those parents are first cousins. Now tell me about the child."

Granny looked for a moment at her hands before answering, "Hat, the boy's feet are turned backwards. I doubt he will ever walk. I pray they will never have other children. What else can I say?" We went home later, not talking, and Granny wasn't her usual self for several days. We went often to check on the mother and child.

At first I was not allowed to see the little boy. I kept asking questions that my grandmother had much difficulty in answering. My constant inquiry was, "Why could this happen if God loves us so much?"

I well remember the Sunday morning when Granny told me at breakfast that we were going to see the baby, and I could hold him. I was excited yet fearful, as I had imagined so many things since hearing Granny tell Aunt Hat about the baby's feet. How would a baby look with feet attached backwards? I began to think I would not go, but Granny was firm and talked of God blessing little children during his time on earth. She held my hand as we walked into the forest and said, "We were given eyes to see the beauty of the earth, ears to hear the voices of others as well as our own, and firm, healthy bodies, but some of those bodies appear to be tainted from the lust of those that have no understanding regarding God's plan for mankind." I shook my head, not understanding the words she spoke.

We arrived with a one-day supply of hippins, as Granny called them, for the new baby, a wee cap and booties Aunt Hat had made, and a jar of fine honey Granny had strained through a piece of cloth that morning. It was almost midday when we stopped within view of the house. We unwrapped two baked sweet potatoes, sat under a large tree, and had our meal.

The lady of the house welcomed us and asked us in without hesitation. Granny inquired about the baby and went over the needed care, feeding, bathing and cleaning of the child's mouth and eyes. When finished, she went over to the crib and gently picked the baby up. She sat in the rocking chair and her free hand reached out to me. "Come, Katherine, see the baby," adding as I stepped forth, "with the mother's permission you can hold him." The small child in Granny's lap appeared to chew on his tiny fist. I touched his fingers, and he grasped my finger and held on. I was surprised at the touch, firm and even. When I tried to withdraw my hand, his clutch was firmer. I looked to Granny. She smiled, and getting up, she seated me in the rocking chair and placed the precious bundle of hippin-bound humanity wrapped in a warm blanket in my arms. I saw nothing but love in the mother's eyes as she spoke to Granny.

"We have named him Will after the man that helped build our cabin. You remember, Granny, he helped you in your harvest several years back. He has the same affliction as Will. We thought it would be honorable."

The blanket had fallen to the side of the chair with a little help from Granny, and for the first time I looked at the wee child's feet and legs. I saw the twisted limbs and the tiny toes that were drawn tightly towards the balls of the feet. I felt the need to touch them, and Granny in her wisdom allowed me to do so.

As we left the cabin I was aware of a feeling I had not had when we arrived. I no longer felt afraid of the many things in life for which we must find meaning and understanding in order to be the person we strive to become.

After a long walk, with several pauses along the way to gather herbs for Granny's cabinet, Aunt Hat was our next stop, and tea and a long talk seemed to be just right. Aunt Hat asked me about the baby, and I told her in great detail about how I had been allowed to hold little Will, how he held onto my finger, not letting go, and how he even smiled. Granny stopped me to say all new babies seem to smile and that this wasn't really a smile. I was disappointed to hear this. I turned to Aunt Hat. "Aunt Hat, Granny said little Will can never walk. Do you think he won't ever walk?"

Aunt Hat looked at Granny, then turned to look into my eyes. After a long few seconds, she took a book from her shelves. While holding the book close to her chest she pointed to a chair. "One word: sit." Then she began, "Granny, remember how you have taught Katherine never to use the word 'can't'? Well, in this book I have just reread several times the facts regarding the bumblebee. His body is too large and his wings are too small for him to fly. He does not know he is not supposed to fly, however, so he flies. Let us all pray that no one ever tells little Will that he cannot walk. He might surprise us."

In a few short years, as Granny made her calls on the mountain people, I was to see Will crawling about in the yard. He was still nursing, as Granny had encouraged the mother to do. In addition, a jar of medicine was given the mother, a tonic, Granny told me. But a lot of soft talking was going on, and for a while when we stopped by Aunt Hat's, she and Granny talked no more of children. I was getting used to the fact that I was not supposed to know everything, just some things necessary for me to know at my age.

CHAPTER 20

The Dusty People

I HAD BEEN with Granny several years and mostly went barefooted during the summer. As it grew cooler and I needed shoes, we discovered that my feet had grown and the shoes I had been wearing last year were too small. Granny stated, "The next passerby going into the high mountain will take word from me that we need a shoemaker, so just go barefooted until the shoemaker gets the word." Since previously my shoes had been purchased in a store or ordered from a catalogue, a shoemaker was something new to me.

I heard Granny's message days later when someone stopped at the spring for a cool drink of water and a meal that Granny offered mountain travelers passing our way. "Will you be going to the high mountain?" she asked.

"Yes'um, I will," the traveler, stated.

"I am in need of a shoemaker," Granny said. The man nodded his head and the message went forth with the messenger.

About two months later on a very cool and crisp morning, a man walked into our yard. He carried a backpack on his back and another leather bag hung from his shoulder. He sat quietly with his head down, waiting for Granny to appear.

I had called to her as usual with, "Granny, someone is here!"

As soon as Granny stepped out of the door, the man rose to his feet, and with head bent low, bowed to her.

"I see you got my message, and I am thankful for your presence," Granny stated in the way expressed by mountain people. A simple thank you was not enough. The man nodded again and waited for instructions regarding Granny's needs. "He also makes other things," Granny had told me, "but shoes are the most desired." Granny suggested the man rest while she prepared food and served it on the porch. After washing his face and hands he proceeded to eat while the food was hot. Granny offered a second helping but he declined.

As he took a black marker from his bag, Granny brought a strip of white cloth she had cut for the measurement of my foot. The shoemaker had me stand on the cloth while he made a black mark around my entire foot, and then asked "How long?" meaning how long do you want the shoes to last?

Granny stated, "One or two years."

He set to work and I watched as he withdrew a shoe last (a metal foot imprint that came in different sizes) from his pack, pieces of leather cut small, and even like strings, then searched for a ball of beeswax. He placed these with all the other things that he used for shoemaking. I watched as he worked away, cutting leather a bit larger than my foot. Before cutting the sides for the shoe, he asked Granny, "High tops?"

Granny gave a slight nod of her head and his work continued.

The shoes took form as I watched in utter amazement as the sheepskin was inserted as the innersole. I tried the first shoe on. Several hours had passed and the sun has gone from high in the sky to almost twilight by the time the shoes were finished and handed to Granny.

With a humble bow and a gesture of thanks for using his service, the two talked of payment. "What do you need?" Granny asked. With head bent, the man spoke without looking up, "Seed corn, honey, and medicine for sores if you have plenty," then added, "only a smidgeon." Granny allowed him to pick what he needs from her supplies. He did not speak as we bid him goodbye.

I couldn't wait to tell Aunt Hat about the new shoes or to ask her about the quiet, timid man that made them. I felt she might know more than Granny did because when I asked, Granny's only words were, "I only know these people as the Dusty People."

Aunt Hat looked at me with a smile, stating, "You are so curious, wanting to know so many things! Don't ever change! This is how one obtains knowledge. Now, what did you think about the man who is only known to the mountain people as the dusty ones?"

I was quick to inform her, "He was handsome, straight and tall, bright blue eyes set in a face that looked as it he had been sprinkled with fine dust." I did not see a full view of his face at any time because his head was low over his work most of the time. However, while working on my shoes and tying them, I got a glimpse of eyes as blue as the sky. His hands looked strong; his fingers much longer than Granny's or Aunt Hat's. He did not say much, and I asked Aunt Hat, "Was he afraid of us?"

Aunt Hat was quiet for a moment and when she began to speak, I was spellbound, "My dear, I believe these people have been mistreated and discriminated against for hundreds of years. I see them as hardworking, productive people. They add so much to our lives here in the mountains and elsewhere." She added after pausing as if in thought, "I know for a fact that many have gone down to Virginia and Kentucky to work in the mines since the start of the Depression, working for a dollar a day, sleeping outside in camps when there was no place to stay. These people are proud, never asking for help from you but always there for you in a kind, gentle, humble way, with head bowed. Not often do they look you straight into your eye. I believe I see some of the pain they've experienced passed from generation to generation. A fine, peace-loving person made your shoes."

She added, "The cloth used to make yours and Granny's dresses was woven on a loom made by the hands of one of these people. Many cabins have such a loom and a spinning wheel. The Dusty People made many of the looms and spinning wheels we use. The homespun materials made by these people are the best, woven tight and strong, and the dye does not wash out or fade. The men make their own tools and plows. The same man that made your shoes cut cedar and let it dry for a year before making the shutters for our cabin windows. In payment, I ordered a handsaw for him from the catalog. The women knit and crochet many household items and work side by side with their husbands. They are such beautiful people. It is unknown when their ancestors came to the mountains or where they came from. I do not believe they are Black-Irish as some say, or that they are of the people of color that fled into the mountains when the slaves were free.

"Granny can tell you these people have a bump on their head; their hair is not coarse. When in a gathering of their own people they speak openly without bowed heads. They are happy, caring and God-fearing, and they take excellent care of their families and elderly members. Like the Indians, they never take more wild deer or other forest animals than they can use. The men walk miles in the forest to find the best seed corn, cuttings of fruit trees and many other things that farmers in the mountain are known to produce. Granny has given them hatching eggs from her hens and the large kernel seed corn that grows well in the high mountains.

"The men wear baggie homespun pants with an over blouse, much like the women wear. They only wear a hat in the winter, and it seems to be made of soft leather of perhaps deer or sheepskin. They own goats and sheep, often seen grazing on the high mountains. One could count on seeing them at the salt lick near Max's Patch Mountain on any given day. The women have long hair, plaited, and more than likely wound around the head. The men do not wear their hair long, however the older men have beards and looked well-kept.

"These people are clean and decent and obey the mountain laws, many of which are of their own making." She went on to say, "I will not be living when society takes time to learn more about these people. Perhaps you will live to see the mountain veil lifted and a people known only as 'The Dusty People' take their rightful place in society, for they have a place, I am sure. Time will enable them to find it."

I asked Granny if I could please spend the night with Aunt Hat. She agreed, so she walked home alone. I stood on the small porch and waved until she was out of sight. I was invited into Aunt Hat's kitchen near suppertime with a wave of her hand. After washing my hands, a knife was given to me. Three turnips were on the dry sink waiting to be peeled and cut into small pieces. I knew a pot of turnip greens had been bubbling away on the stove for some time. The three turnips were added to the turnip greens with several herb leaves from the garden outside.

I helped with the corn dumplings, made much like cornbread with one exception: the milk was heated before mixing with the meal, flour, salt and rising powder, known as baking powder. The reason for heating the milk is to hold the flour and meal together when dropped in the boiling liquid. Then the mixture is dropped by the spoonful into the cooked turnip greens. I was instructed not to add too many at a time, to allow them to rise to the top first, then push them aside and add more. The liquid in the pot was called "pot liquor".

We enjoyed the meal consisting of two pork chops; we shared a large baked sweet potato and helped ourselves to butter from a small crock taken from the springhouse. Pork chops were a special treat, as most mountain people did not eat meat daily; some only once a week on the Sabbath.

After watching the stars, Aunt Hat rocked in the rocking chair on the porch, and I sat on the steps and wondered about the many people watching the stars just as we were.

CHAPTER 21

The Pot Mender

A TYPICAL MORNING began with the rooster announcing the coming of dawn and the new calf calling for his mother. I heard hens as they flew from their roosting places in the chicken house, and one morning, to my surprise, my ears caught a sound not familiar to me. It was the clanking of a bell. I quickly went to waken Granny, but she had been up for some time. I rushed into the kitchen.

"I hear a bell, Granny, do you hear it too?"

She smiled that reassuring smile and said, "Yes, the ole' pot mender came by late last night, you were in bed sleeping. I let him rest for the night in the barn. He will have breakfast on the porch as soon as it's ready. Don't go outside without me, Katherine, until he leaves. He's someone I don't know, we must be careful."

I nodded my head, but before long I found myself opening the shutter and taking a peek. He had a cart loaded with pots and pans and many other things I didn't recognize. He was feeding a large billy goat, and as I watched, he prepared to hitch the goat to the cart. As the goat moved about, a large bell around his neck rang. I stayed inside as Granny called to the man, telling him she had prepared breakfast for him. He thanked her, sat quietly on the bench, took the plate, and bowed his head in prayer before eating.

I saw that a good plate of food had been prepared for him, with eggs, sausage, grits or cornmeal mush. I couldn't tell for sure because we had yellow meal and yellow grits, whichever we had ground at the time. Yellow or white corn was used, whichever we had the most of. I watched Granny as she spread butter on large slabs of bread she had just taken from the oven. She cut ham she kept in the safekeeper, put this in a cloth bag, and carried it to the porch.

"Take care," she stated, "I wish you well. Our pots do not need mending this time; however, come by the next time you are in our neck of the woods. We will see."

The man took the food, bowed his head, and quickly stepped down from the porch, took the lead line, and walked away. The old goat seemed to know just what was expected of him. Off they went into the early morning mist, as I, a young girl, watched from behind an open shutter in my grandmother's cabin.

I turned to ask, "Will they be all right, Granny?"

"It's up to them, child," she said. "They are working, so I think they will both be back again. You can't keep working people down, Katherine. They fall, but get up, and start right away to finish what they started."

I really thought about that a lot the next few days. Life was so hard in the mountains, but then God had given these mountain people so much beauty, such breathtaking views of valleys, majestic trees, vines that climbed as far up as one can see, sunsets that were beyond comparison, winds that caressed your entire being, and cool rain that so often replenished the earth.

I have now come to believe what Granny meant when she said, "We are all cut from the same bolt of cloth," meaning there is no difference in any of us, only the way we think. That is where the difference is. Another lesson in life. I learned new lessons every day and loved all of it. My time there was well-spent. Please, God, don't let me forget, not even one lesson.

CHAPTER 22

Granny Breaks Her Arm
and
More Trauma in My Young Life

THE HAYING SEASON came and I worked like a man, raking hay in windrows with a horse and rake, which I could handle as well as anyone. The hay had been cut three days earlier, and I raked it into long rows, and then we hauled it to the barn in a wagon. The hardest part at haying time was pitching hay into the wagon and then unloading it in the barn because this time the hay had to be pitched high into the barn loft. This was backbreaking work. Some days I found it necessary to roll out of bed onto my knees before straightening up. Every muscle was stiff and sore. I wondered how my grandmother could work as hard as she did with no ill effects. Granny was over eighty years old but never complained, and there were very few mornings in her home that she did not awaken without a song.

On the final day of haying other people came to help us finish our work, as they had all of their own hay under cover of the loft. We worked until noon and the last load of hay had been pitched into the barn loft. Everyone had brought a basket of food, as was the custom. We ate, talked and laughed, and Granny asked me to play the guitar while we all sang. The singing lasted for hours, and everyone had fun. Even I could laugh. I laughed so much that night, my sides hurt, and Granny threatened to give me croton oil, which was a vile-tasting medicine used to cure a stomachache.

The next morning, I awakened to the sound of rain on the tin roof, and I remember feeling so glad we'd gotten the hay in. It rained for days, and the valleys were flooded. One night, a man came for Granny. He told her of a neighbor whose husband's leg had been crushed in a bridge washout while he was trying to get to his family. Granny packed a few things in a bag, and we left quickly to assist them.

Only two miles from our place, we found we could not cross the creek. The water was out of bounds. As we turned to go back, the man pulled the horse too sharply to one side and the buggy overturned. I was thrown clear, but my grandmother was pinned underneath. We worked with a long pole to get the buggy off of her. After walking back in the rain, I found my grandmother had broken her left arm. She'd not said one word about it during the two-mile walk. She showed me how to fix a splint of thin hickory slates and how to wrap the arm after it was set. Then she wrapped a linen tea towel around the second rung of a kitchen chair, which she instructed me to turn upside down. After telling me to hold the chair firmly, she placed the linen towel around her arm and added pressure by pulling back and giving her arm a quick twist. I heard the bone as it slipped into place. She then gave me directions regarding the splint and wrappings, which I applied as she instructed, wrapping and unwrapping several times until it finally met with her approval.

This extraordinary person insisted on going to the barn that night to help me milk the two cows! I can still see her on the milking stool, bucket between her knees, milking with one hand, and she finished long before I did.

Granny's broken arm did not slow this lady up for long. In less than a week, she was down the mountainside with a basket of food for someone in need. I begged to be allowed to stay at home because I was learning to play the organ, which, according to Granny, she'd been given in exchange for twenty bushels of corn. After extracting a

PEARL K. MCCULLOUGH

promise that I would not go into the woods or off the place, she set off on her errand of mercy.

I played the organ for some time, carried in wood, made a fire to prepare dinner, and then decided to surprise Granny with a cake. She had taught me to cook and bake almost as well as any of the mountain folk, and I knew the recipe for a pound cake: Use one pound of each ingredient: sugar, flour, butter, milk, and eggs. Add a bit of vanilla, and you have a wonderful cake. I didn't have enough eggs in the house, so I went to the barn and looked in all the wooden boxes we had nailed on the inside wall for nests. I had my apron full of eggs, two or three dozen, when I heard a hen cackling in the loft. I put the eggs down in one of the boxes and climbed to the top of the ladder, looking over as much of the loft as I could see from my position. I saw what I thought to be places where hens would nest; one hen came out of the corner still cackling. I took the pitchfork in my hand and walked across the loft. As I stood in the sweet-smelling hay, I heard a mockingbird singing in the distance, and through the hay door I saw white puffs of cloud that seemed to play hide and seek over the mountains.

Suddenly I felt a chill go over my body, and I was afraid. I turned to go back across the loft and saw a boy standing between me and the ladder. I recognized him as one of the boys who had helped us during haying season. I tried to speak, but my vocal cords were paralyzed. He told me he did not intend to hurt me. I asked him to step aside and let me pass, but he only laughed and told me to give him the pitchfork. I tried to run to the hay door, but the hay was deep and hard to run in. He caught me and threw me to the floor of the loft. I fought until I was breathless, and I cried out for mercy. I even told him I had been raped before and to please not put me through this again. I kept trying to talk him out of this ungodly act, and he began to beat me in the face. I stopped fighting and let him have his way. I knew that if I didn't, he would kill me. When he threatened me with motherhood, I fainted.

When I opened my eyes I was alone. Bruised and battered, I made my way down the ladder and into the barnyard. I stumbled to the water trough where I had so often splashed my face with cool water. I tried to wash the blood from my face, and I was weeping uncontrollably, when suddenly I felt Granny's hand on my head. I couldn't look her in the face. I lied and tried to tell her I had fallen out of the barn loft, but oh, Granny, dear, sweet Granny was too wise for that. I guess my eyes showed my suffering. She knew me so well and could look into the depths of my being.

"Who was it, child?" she asked softly. "Now, we're not having two or three years of silence over this, are we?"

When I remained silent, she took my hand and led me into the house and to my bed. I was bathed and cared for, and then with her one good arm she gently pressed me to her breast and whispered against my hair, "Now, dear, tell Granny all about it, and we'll never talk of this again. But you must not keep this inside your heart. Get it out of your innards and then forget it."

So I told my grandmother every word I could remember, of begging, pleading for mercy, and even calling out to God for help. Then I told her the boy's name. She half bowed her head and I heard her say, "Lord, have mercy."

Granny made me a strong cup of herb tea and told me to drink it all down. She stood solemnly by as I drained it. When I handed her the empty cup, she covered me with a large lap robe and told me to sleep. As she stooped to kiss me, several tears splashed on my face. I watched as she slowly went to the gun rack over the mantle and took the gun down. I begged her not to leave the house and would have tried to stop her, but I couldn't raise my body from the couch.

I must have slept the clock around. Several times I awakened and tried to sit up, only to fall back on my bed and sleep again. After a long time I opened my eyes to see Granny busy preparing food and doing her usual chores. When I tried to talk to her about her whereabouts, she was quick to tell me I had been dreaming. I could see the gun in the rack and thought perhaps I had indeed been dreaming, so the discussion was dropped.

A few days later, several men stopped by the house and asked Granny if she had seen any sign of bears lately.

"No," she replied, "I haven't, but that doesn't mean there haven't been any. I've been too busy to look for signs of bears. Why do you ask?"

One of the men answered Granny by saying that one of the neighbor's boys was sent to bring the cows home and he hadn't been seen in three days. His folks were worried that something had happened to him. They thought perhaps a bear had attacked him and dragged his body through the woods. "But if you haven't seen any signs," the man finished, "we'll look in another area."

I held my breath as I heard Granny say, "Well, I feel sorry for the family. Sorry I can't go over to be with the missus to comfort her, but I have a sick granddaughter here. She fell out of the barn loft a few days ago when she was frightened by a skunk, and she hurt herself pretty badly."

"Yes," one man went on to say, "that could be rather frightening."

"Well," replied Granny as she washed her hands in the basin on the back porch, then dried them on her apron, "that skunk's frightening days are over."

The laughing men left to look for the lost boy.

He was found three months later, ten miles from home. He had fallen over a cliff near Blowing Rock, North Carolina.

I knew by then that I was with child.

CHAPTER 23

Overnight A Child Becomes A Woman

I HAD BEEN suffering from morning sickness. I wanted to talk with Granny about this, but I was ashamed, so I tried to steal away and be by myself as much as possible in the forest. I believe with all my heart that Granny would have done anything in her power to help me if only I had confided in her. I had watched her concoct several potions to stay the quickening of unwanted life in our livestock and other animals. I knew she had given our dog a mixture of this same remedy at one time when she had been exposed to a male while still a puppy herself. Granny had said the dog was too young to have puppies. I knew the jar was on the shelf with Flossy's name on it.

That night I made a strong cup of tea from this mixture, and after getting down on my knees in front of my bed, I said, "God, I asked You for help while I was being raped by this boy. I cried and pleaded with You for mercy. Is this mercy? I need Your help, because I am taking this medicine knowing fully that I will be destroying an unwanted life. If I am doing wrong, forgive me. You haven't given me strength to protect myself from those who hurt me, but I am learning to survive by my wits, and knowing of nothing else to do, I am drinking it down, even if it kills me!"

Later, when the cramps grew more intense I hurried into the forest just back of Granny's cabin. I felt warm body fluid running down my legs and covering my feet. I stopped for breath as sharp pains continued to shoot through my body, as if driven by a force not known by me. I remember thinking I thought I knew every pain that could ever be imagined or felt by anyone. But no, this was a new pain, a pain that was to remain with me for the next thirty-five years of my life. For now, each time I see the smiling face of a child, or hear the laughter of children at play, the pain within my heart makes itself known. I cried softly that night, not weeping for the life I was destroying, but for the many children who would find themselves in the same circumstances and be forced to make the same decision I felt I must make.

The smell of blood filled my nostrils and caused me to feel faint as I sank to the ground. It crossed my mind more than once that this might well attract wild animals, which made me even more afraid. I was wearing a long nightgown Granny had made for me with Aunt Hat's help, and I was bare footed. The sticky blood clung to the lower part of my body as I pushed the gown between my legs and tried to hold it there, using both hands to stop the bleeding. Some time passed before a large blood clot was expelled and the bleeding lessened. I leaned back against a large tree in a sitting position, and there I remained for a very long time. I knew I must get back to the cabin before Granny awoke and set out to look for me.

I walked a short distance, but then returned, putting my hands on the ground to find the damp place where I sank to the ground. With my hands drenched with blood I dug a sizeable hole, pushed the damp soil and leaves into the hole atop the blood clot, then gently patted the soil back into place as I had so often watched my Granny do when planting seeds. I was not quite thirteen years old, but I knew I was leaving the seed of life in the forest, and my heart was full of sorrow. As I returned to the cabin, I thought I would die. A part of me actually did die then, and I have lived my entire life remembering this night.

I awakened Granny and told her what had taken place while she slept. As usual, she took me into her arms and let me cry, knowing

I'd had to grow up fast. She realized, though words were not spoken, that two lives had been taken that night.

I didn't think I would ever be able to help anyone else, but just as the sun was rising there in the beautiful North Carolina forest, I promised Granny, on my knees, that if the need should ever arise, I would make myself available to help another in need.

Granny wrapped me in a heavy blanket and sat me on a chamber pot half filled with boiling water mixed with her special herbs from the shed room. She repeated this procedure several time a day for a week or more. This treatment was to prevent what Granny called "child birth fever." I was not to use the outside privy, I later learned, because Granny was afraid I would get an infection, very prevalent with miscarriages. How fortunate I was to have dear Granny to watch over me and nurse me back to health.

I never again went into that part of the woods where I washed away my childhood tears and took on the responsibility of a woman.

Afterwards

After that, I frequently awakened in the early morning hours, but only partially, confused thoughts intermixing with bad dreams. Again and again I relived the same painful experience as in my mind I went into the forest and looked around me. There was the beautiful tree I sat under for so long in such pain and sorrow. There, the log with green moss and soil that covered part of the small grave bearing my sorrow. A little lizard came forth from the hollowed-out log and blinked at me with a startled look. The gray squirrel barked as if warning me not to intrude, then settled down again, cracked a nut. He seemed to understand that I was not a stranger but a part of the landscape that I, too, had claimed as my own. We were pieces of fabric woven together by a weaver on a magical loom. The tapestry blended into wondrous colors, the shuttle flew back and forth, and my thoughts, pain and sorrow were woven within.

PEARL K. MCCULLOUGH

What was to become of me? Where would I find peace? If not here, where? I could see no future for me there, I could not face the past, not for one moment, so I must pretend it hadn't happened; then perhaps it would be like the bunny that lost his long tail that Granny told me about. He was thrown into the briar patch with only a stump of his tail after he lost the main part, and he got out fine and went merrily on his way. How strange that I should think of that story at that time.

Perhaps there is a reason, I thought. I sat up, locked my arms around my knees, listened with a keen ear to the song of the winds, felt the warm morning sun on my back, raised my face to the sky and sought comfort in the dense growth that Mother Nature provided so abundantly. I sought peace, and, yes, after a time I found what I had been searching for. Walking away, no trail left behind me, my footprints faded as the rich mountain soil slowly fell to cover them. A child became a woman that night when she shed the dress of childhood, draped her adult cloak over her shoulders, and walked stumbling in bare feet into the school of life

CHAPTER 24

Hunting, Shooting

GRANNY TAUGHT ME to shoot a rifle and I was a good shot, but I was taught not to kill anything we could not eat, and then only as much as we needed. Never should a deer or another animal be left in the woods to suffer if I made a bad shot. When this happened, I was to look for the animal and put an end to its suffering.

One day I shot a deer and he fell, but when I climbed up the hill, he was nowhere in sight. I found blood on the ground, but I could not pick up his trail any further. I ran for Granny in a panic, and she came to help me. She looked around the spot where I said he had fallen and showed me the crushed leaves, fresh overturned bits of debris and then about ten paces down the other side of the hill, she called to me and showed me a pressed-down place in the leaves. Blood was on the bushes, and Granny picked up one leaf and studied it closely.

"Let's go," she said, without looking at me. "You have made a lung shot, and that poor critter is suffering."

We hurried on to find the deer. Sure enough, there he was under some bushes, breathing hard, with blood foaming from his mouth. Granny took my gun and killed him. I just didn't have the heart.

She showed me where the bullet had gone clear through his lungs, in one side of his body and out the other side. I wanted to know how she knew he had been lung-shot. "Just remember, any time you see foaming blood from an animal, you have shot him in the lungs. If he's still on his feet, find him and put an end to his suffering. God doesn't intend to have his creatures suffer."

CHAPTER 25

Snowed In—Rescued by the Mountain People

O N A COLD winter night, with snow deep on the ground and winds racing around the corners of Granny's house, we sat before a grand fire, toasted our toes and often our backsides as we stood and held our skirts above our knees, allowing the fire to warm our bodies. How safe and secure we both felt at this time.

In January the days began dark and dreary. Granny had been worried about a hard winter. We toted in wood day after day until the shed room was so full, one could hardly walk around. We brought water from the well and stored it in wooden barrels. Our dried fruit and vegetables were stored in the kitchen. Both sweet and Irish potatoes were brought in from the mounds of soil and pine needles in the garden where they were usually stored and put on the floor, covered with sacks and horse blankets.

We were so busy getting our cabin ready for whatever was to happen, I did not have time to complain about being tired. The pickled beans, kraut, pickled corn, and all the other things were put near the kitchen, and finally we had a few hours of rest.

About noon the following day, Granny climbed the ladder into the loft room and brought down an armful of candles she'd made some time before, and quietly put them in a large basket, dusted off her hands, looked around, and nodded her head.

We had a short walk in the forest the next day, as Granny did not want to get too far from the cabin. I asked her why she thought we would have a hard winter.

"Just look at the insects," she said, "the nests are high, even the hornets' nests are higher up in the trees. They're not using the ground nests. The yellow jackets have built nests in the trees this year, too. The woolly worms are light brown and dark brown, that's a sure sign. And can you beat this?" she asked me. "The squirrels are storing nuts in our loft room! A bad winter will arrive soon, and all the creatures seem to know this."

Sure enough it did arrive. Two days later ten inches of snow covered the ground. I was not allowed out, so Granny went alone to feed and water the stock. She returned after milking our cow to tell me the chickens did not leave the roost to eat. She said she had turned the calf in with the cow, fed the hogs and the horse, and put water in the watering trough.

We had breakfast, and the rest of that day I watched it snow. We could not see the barn clearly. Granny called this a blizzard. "Mountain folks fear times like this," she stated, knowing that probably some would not survive.

The second day, snow was several feet deep and Granny could not feed or water the livestock. She tried twice to clear a path to the barn but was unable to do so. We had supper by the fire that night. Often a large puff of smoke came down the chimney and we were showered with sparks. The wind blew so hard, I began to cry, and Granny comforted me and assured me we would be all right.

Some hours later the wind eased, but the snow did not let up during the night. The next morning was no different, and we soon found ourselves completely snowed in. When Granny saw me standing in amazement with my hand to my mouth, she came and gave me a hug, putting my mind at ease.

"Sit down, child, let's have some hot mush and then we will have a special day, playing games that I played as a child." The mush tasted smooth and sweet as I watched for a sign of fear in the eyes of this fearless lady of the mountains I knew as my Granny.

PEARL K. MCCULLOUGH

I shall always remember the games we played that day. Granny tried to keep me busy, and I knew she did not want me to be concerned about us being snowed in. We played such games as tic tac toe; marbles on the game table; throwing a ball of twine for distance (whoever threw the ball the longest distance ten times was the winner); holding a bean on your nose and walking around the room with your head up high; closing your eyes, then trying to touch your nose; raising your legs one at a time to see how long you could hold this position; breathing deeply, then holding your breath as long as you could; scooting across the room on your backside three times without stopping; clapping your hands and legs in a drum-like cadence; counting dried beans in a jar (the one that had guessed the right amount of beans previously placed in the jar by the other one was the winner). We played these games for hours.

I was wondering if anyone would come to see about us, and finally I asked Granny, "How do you know someone will come?"

She smiled that reassuring smile and said, "The mountain people take care of each other, dear, you will see. We are safe in our cabin and God is with us; we have nothing to fear."

I wasn't so sure. The snow was so deep, but our cabin was warm and comfortable. I was somewhat worried about our wood supply giving out or the roof falling in, but not Granny. She kept repeating, "All is well, just know all is well. Always remember, child, everything is on its way somewhere. The river as it flows often rises beyond its banks; the wind as it blows sways the trees back and forth; the rain as it sweeps like a broom on land in need of a soaking; the stars as they slowly glide across the sky and twinkle in merriment as they nod to other stars passing by; the snow as it caresses the bare trees and lands on cabin roofs just like ours, and perhaps causing much concern by humans who most likely are easily alarmed.

"Why, child, we have not been harmed! There is a reason for all these goings on. Let's just wait; be thankful and you'll see. And as I said, Katherine, everything is on its way somewhere, so don't fret. Let's enjoy our games together and time will pass; our friends will come and help us. We can be assured of that."

At that point I knew my Granny was right, as she always was. I pulled my knees up to my chin and sat daydreaming before our fire, watching as burning logs leapt with warm flames, and their sparks flew up the chimney going somewhere. Yes, I thought, everything is on its way somewhere.

I was kept so busy I had no time for fear. And then, late in the afternoon we heard a voice, and Granny walked to the door. When she opened the door, snow fell into the room because the wind from last night had blown huge snow piles onto the porch.

Four men were in the yard. They had arrived in a homemade sled with runners on it, much like a wagon without wheels, but much smaller. Two horses pulled the sled.

Greeting Granny, they told her they had come as soon as possible.

They went to work at once feeding the stock, taking care of things in the barn, and cleaning the muck from the horse and cow stalls. Most of the chickens had died; they had fallen off the roosts, frozen.

The men then took from the barn loft a long thin piece of lumber with two holes in each end. Several feet of rope were pushed through these holes, and this was used to scrape the snow from the roof. A man on each end pushed the snow, and I watched from the window as the roof's snow came down to rest against our cabin, growing higher by the minute.

I didn't realize Granny and I had been almost buried in this white death that mountain people feared so much.

This work went on for more hours than I can remember. When all was in order, the men left and returned three more times before the storm ended. Granny was so grateful, and needless to say, so was I. This kind, gentle lady reminded me, "We all need each other." She was always there for her people, and they in turn were never far away when she needed them.

PEARL K. MCCULLOUGH

CHAPTER 26

Strangers in our Woods: Febbie and Annie Laurel

DURING A WINTER'S evening as we shelled dried peas, throwing the empty shells into the burning fire, I noticed Granny's work-worn hands and said something about it. She laughed, and said her hands had been involved in too many chores to really remember. Oh yes, they have worked with life and with death.

"Did I ever tell you about little Annie Laurel?" she asked. I shook my head, knowing I was about to hear a wee bit more of Granny's life in the mountains.

She went on to say, "One day while gathering sassafras roots, I came upon two men building a cabin several miles up near Max Patch Mountain. I stopped and asked, "Who's going to live there?"

"Don't know," was the answer.

"I let it go for a while, knowing I would learn the answer sooner or later. News is slow here, but does get around," she said quietly.

I pondered in my heart and waited with baited breath, as I knew another happening was formulating in Granny's mind. "I did hear later that a lawman from Hot Springs, North Carolina had bought a small parcel of land here, was having a cabin built, and had agreed to give it back to the family he bought it from in ten years. Often in the early fall I saw a young woman walking in the forest. I would wave to her or nod my head, and she in return seemed to accept my greeting, but quickly looked away. Needless to say, by this time heads were turning, necks were craning, and lips were flapping as everyone wondered what was going on. Mountain people like to know those in their midst. Of course I knew," said Granny, stopping her pea shelling for a moment. "This young girl was in the family way. She was so beautiful, yet frail and puny. Some time after that when I saw the mailman, he told me her name was Febbie Laurel, and she sure got a lot of mail. I told him she was a nice neighbor, although I thought to myself later, I didn't even know her.

"Months passed, and frequently I saw Febbie walking or sitting under a tree with a book in her hand, but I did not violate her space.

"I was cleaning the horse trough the day the mailman came up the hill pretty much excited," Granny said, with her head nodding. "Yes, he sure was. 'You better look in on the woman in the new cabin, she hasn't picked up her mail in some time,' he said. 'I went by, she won't come to the door.'

"I flew to the house, grabbed a few things I would need, including some elm bark water, and set off at a half run for the cabin. When I arrived, there was no sign of life, so I just lifted the latch and walked right in. The woman was crossways in the bed, legs drawn up to her large stomach, hands holding a pillow to her chest and face. She did not say one word, and neither did I. The one-room cabin was clean, and the pine floor shined as sunbeams danced around. I opened the window, drew in a deep breath, and set about preparing for the birthing. Going to the bed, I whispered, 'I'm here to help you.' She gave me a weak smile, drew her thin lips over her clenched teeth, and nodded her head.

"About twenty-four hours later, she gave birth to a beautiful baby girl. She did not cry or scream as many women do when birthing. She only said two words in twenty-four hours. I heard them clearly: 'Andrew, Andrew.'

"After the birthing I cleaned the child, washed her eyes with the elm bark water, wrapped her in a warm blanket, and placed her in her mother's arms. She unwrapped the little one and looked over her

PEARL K. MCCULLOUGH

entire body with a mother's love. She seemed to be counting those tiny fingers and toes."

My own heart was racing as Granny told this part of the story. My body was wet, clammy, and I felt a knife had just pierced my heart. I tried not to let Granny know how I felt or what was going on in my young mind. I closed my eyes for a moment and tried with every ounce of my being not to think of the night I walked into the forest barefooted to rid my body of my own baby. I wondered, will I ever feel as Febbie did when she counted those little fingers and toes?

Grandma saw my reaction to her story and asked, "Are you all right, Katherine?"

"Oh yes Granny," I answered, "please go on. What about the baby's name?"

As Granny continued, I sat there unable to move and absorbed in every word, even as my heart cried silently.

"'I'm Febbie', the girl told me, speaking slowly. 'I think we should call her Annie, Ann Laurel if that's all right with you?'

'Right as rain,' I said with gladness, as I tidied up the room. I thought she would need someone for a few days, and how Aunt Hat would be good for her and little Annie.

"Land's sake, I haven't seen as many books in my life as Febbie had in that cabin: books on shelves, books in every space. I knew Aunt Hat would love this, she too being a book lover. There were baby books with covers of mother and child, and enough clothes for five little ones, and I couldn't help but wonder, where was the father? Well, it was no concern of mine; I must let matters be.

"Aunt Hat was so happy to be a part of these goings on, you would think she had died and gone to the happy hunting ground. She arrived with a few things in hand, including teapot, tea, knitting needles, and her tatting that she was busy with when she had time on her hands.

"I went over often. We sat outside under one of the trees and talked. Aunt Hat had gone home by then, and Febbie and little Annie were on their own. They did not seem to want for anything. Their needs were few. They lived a simple life; they had mail often, I was told. One could tell at a glance, happiness for them was contentment and seclusion. I watched as little Annie grew taller each spring and fall over the next four or five years. I noticed too that she spoke as her mother did, 'proper,' as mountain folk say. She walked with her head high, back straight, and her laughter rang out as the wind carried it afar."

"Where is little Annie now, Granny?" I asked.

"One day I went by the cabin," said Granny, "everything was gone, Febbie, little Annie, all the books and household things. One thing was left, a note in the cabin room. "Thank you," it read, "whoever reads this, know that you are loved."

CHAPTER 27

Memories of My Mother

WITH SUCH THOUGHTS in mind of motherhood, I thought of my own mother and set to remembering days gone by. I found myself in my favorite place in the forest, my feet in a cool mountain stream, my young mind thinking of my gentle mother, and me being at home as a child. I traced each step she made and often hugged her legs as she went about her daily chores. I heard her sing those songs she loved and hum to herself, asking all of us children to join her. She was a loving mother.

One day Granny told me a short story about a mother rabbit and how she hid her babies in the tall grass to protect them from danger. I was thinking my mother was a protector to her children. Oh, how I remembered when she died. Several days before her death she called each child to her bed and put her loving, gentle hands on our foreheads. Her words are imbedded forever in my heart and mind: "Lord, I can no longer care for these children. You gave them to me only on loan. I now return them to You. Please care for them as You have for me." And then one morning we were awakened and all seven of us were taken to the living room and told that our dear mother had died at 12:10 the night before.

Tears of sadness trickled down onto my dress and shoes. I knew, of course, that on this earth I would never see my mother again. However, she had spoken of heaven almost daily, and I knew in my heart she was at peace without pain, and that was in itself comforting. I heard a bird as he sang his own song, and this one seemed to sing "cheer up, cheer up." I got to my feet, threw a kiss to the bird, and ran home to Granny, who was there to wipe away my tears.

The hills were alive with flaming color. Each tree stood tall and majestic in the crisp morning air. I stopped and listened on a rise for the early morning sounds: the birds busy with their songs, the squirrel barking for his mate, and far off on the second rise, I heard a cock crowing and somewhere another cock answered. How beautiful was my world! How long I was to remember this day. How many times in the next ten years was I to let my mind wander back over this early morning walk, and thank God because He had allowed me this part of my life with Granny and all the lovely things of the beautiful North Carolina forest that gave so much and expected so little in return.

That morning I felt close to my mother. I remembered her asking God to take care of His children, and I wondered why she had not asked God to take care of *her* children. *Was I really one of God's children?* I asked myself. Does God have problem children? My father had so often called me that, saying, "What does one do with a problem child?" I thought if God had lots of Grannies like mine, He would have ample help with all His problem children.

I rushed over the green hills with a song in my heart and wings of happiness attached to my feet, down the deep valley, covered with mountain laurel, honeysuckle and sweet fern, tumbling over in the last few feet into fresh smelling clover, looking up into a clear blue sky. I picked a reed and tasted the goodness within its thin stem. I stared straight up while lying on my back, and started thinking: *Where is God?* I asked myself that question over and over for the next few years, but that night when I asked Granny, "Where is God?" she put her fork down quietly and covered my small hand with her large one.

"Why, child, have you never been taught that God is within you?"

I did not understand this for years. I'd run away searching for love and a feeling of being wanted and needed, and all that while I had the one thing in my heart and life that I needed to bind up my broken heart and spirit, for surely the Kingdom of God is within us.

CHAPTER 28

Heaven's Green Canopy;
Granny Reaches Out to Me

A S IT WAS not a day of work, I wasn't fully awake when
Granny rousted me out of bed, stating, "Today is a fine day,
not a cloud in the sky. The earth is still warm, so let's go to the high
mountain once more before winter."

"Have I been there?" I asked, thinking of the many places I'd seen
while tracking behind Granny.

"No, this is a new place for you."

Off we went, walking hour after hour. We stopped often to rest
and I looked in amazement as the trees got taller, greener and so
thick that one seemed lost in the vastness of the forest that had now
become a wall of trees and vegetation. We finally came to a clearing
and I saw the most beautiful sight my eyes would ever behold. The
clearing likened to a large emerald, perfect in shape and density. The
grass was cool to my bare feet; the ferns were tall and appeared to
laugh with the breeze as it gently pulled them back and forth. A large
tree had fallen on the edge of the clearing, and there we sat to rest.

Granny signaled me to be still and pointed to a rotten log not
far away. A mother bear with two cubs was digging at the log. We
watched, not moving as she rolled the log over and then dug up soft
soil and the cubs ate. Granny held my hand as we sat and watched
the bear family enjoying their meal. The mother bear raised her
head, sniffed the air, then she and the cubs scurried away. Granny
told me they would not harm us unless we were a threat; they were
hunting for grub worms, large white worms that are plentiful in the

rich mountain forest. The mother bear had picked up our scent and had taken her cubs out of danger.

I could not speak for a few minutes; I was so impressed with my surroundings. I had not asked Granny one question since arriving here. I saw that she looked my way several times as if to say, *what are you thinking?* When the sun was near mid afternoon by Granny's timetable, she raised her hand to her brow and looked at the sun. I knew the time had come when we must descend the high mountain. I wondered why we came. Was Granny in her wisdom showing me something that few, only the mountain people, get to see?

I watched as Granny pulled a bag from the folds of her shirt and placed it under a rock near the trunk of the fallen tree, then changed her mind, picked up the bag again and tied it on one of the branches that still clung to the tree. She used one of her shoestrings to tie two knots in the strings. Then she looked around once more before taking my hand, and led me around the fallen tree and back down the mountain. I knew what was in this bag, seeds I had helped Granny gather. There were seed onions, beans, corn, tomato seeds, and many other seeds. However, who was here to use them? I finally got up enough courage to ask Granny. The only thing she said was, "Someone is living up here in the high mountains. I know not why, but I must help them to survive. I have been doing this for four years. As long as someone takes the seeds, I will provide them." Granny's look told me the time had arrived for me to say no more.

The next day my legs were in knots and I had to do stretching exercises to get them to perform properly. Meanwhile, Granny went about the chores as usual, with no pain or cramps. This I found utterly amazing.

CHAPTER 29

A Heartbreaking Decision

ALTHOUGH I LOVED Granny dearly, I realized I was no longer happy living in the mountains. Too much had happened, and I felt a strong force pulling me to I knew not where. By this time I had lived with Granny for five and a half years, and now at thirteen and a half, I wanted to get an education more than anything else.

I loved Granny and everyone in the mountain community that had come into my life, but I could not endure the thought of living in such isolation from the rest of the outside world. I knew I could never spend the rest of my life there.

I began with a simple statement to this strange but special person whom I had come to love and respect. "Granny, when the weather warms in the spring, I'm leaving the mountains."

Shaking her head, she told me, "You are not ready to go off on your own. You cannot get a job, what will you do? You are just a child."

I reminded Granny, "Aunt Hat said many times that you can be what you want to be."

Granny shook her head and said, "Aunt Hat did not mean this would happen in a few weeks or months, Katherine. This takes years of training, studying and serious planning. We will talk with Aunt Hat, and she can teach you to be patient. I won't have you going off on your own, you're still a child."

To please Granny I agreed to spend more time with Aunt Hat; however, I felt I knew enough about life to survive on my own.

What I didn't know was how painful breaking away from the mountains and their inhabitants would be, most particularly Granny.

Aunt Hat welcomed me when I was placed in her tender care with two changes of clothing and another cocoon that Granny had found in the forest. We began reading for hours on end, talked until past midnight every night, and soon after breakfast each day the whole process started again. Aunt Hat reminded me that Granny had sacrificed so much for me, had endangered her future and even her very life for me.

"Your Granny would go the last mile for you. I wonder if you will ever know the heartache she has been struggling with these past years." I knew then that Aunt Hat was aware of the terrible episode in the barn loft and of Granny's efforts to help me.

I returned to Granny's cabin after several days, but visited Aunt Hat several times a month and often spent two or three nights studying with her, her watchful eye and gentle voice guiding and encouraging me.

Over the years during the long winter months, Granny had taught me a certain amount of arithmetic using hickory nuts. She spread them out on the kitchen table and had me take away so many, then count the ones left, then divide them in groups. In this fashion she taught me to add, take away, and multiply. Granny never went to school a day in her life, but she sure knew a lot. She knew I had to be somewhat prepared before going off on my own, and all those years she had been doing just that. Finally she came to realize I most likely could take care of myself. I looked and acted older than I really was, and she finally came to understand my need to start my life anew elsewhere.

CHAPTER 30

Time to Leave

EARLY ONE SPRING morning I awoke in the early hours before dawn with a sinking feeling deep in my chest. It was the day I must convince my dear Granny that I must leave the mountains in hope of finding my purpose for living. I saw that Granny was already at prayer on her knees near her bed, so I went to kneel beside her. She took my hand and we bowed our heads and prayed in silence.

At breakfast I told Granny that it was time for me to leave. She cried and begged me to stay at least until I was sixteen. I shook my head and rose from my chair and walked outside. Granny quickly followed, pulling me close to her heart as we sank to the ground, holding on to each other. We remained in this state for some time, both weeping openly, our tears flowing freely.

As we regained our composure we looked deep into each other's eyes and saw that neither of us had changed our mind.

"Let's walk," Granny stated, getting her large walking stick that she always placed near the door.

I followed her, and soon I was in step with this "walking lady of the mountains" as she was known to many.

We did not talk for some time as we passed through the sweet smelling ferns, mountain laurel, fennel, and so many other plants so delightful to look at, all covered with dew. I was always tempted to pluck these plants, taking the fragrance with me.

We finally stopped and sat beneath our favorite tree. Granny told me she had hoped I would be willing to stay with her and learn the healing ways of the mountain people. She explained to me that mothers, grandmothers, and great-grandmothers passed to special daughters the mountain methods of healing or treatment of people and animals. She said, "You, my child, could take my place when I am no longer here."

"Oh, Granny, I couldn't!" I cried. "What do I know?"

"I will help you," Granny replied. "This is how knowledge is passed on. You have been learning from the first day you climbed the mountain. You have learned much about plants, herbs, and treatment of people and animals. Aunt Hat believes you are a good thinker. She, like me, hopes and prays that you will not leave us."

Granny went about plucking different plants and herbs, having me name each one, then she handed me a double handful of soil she had just that moment scooped from the rich mountain forest floor. She pressed it into my hand. "This is where we both belong," she says. "We are such a part of everything here. Child, you were born here, you have come home, please do not leave. You will be safer with me. That world that awaits you can bring nothing but heartache and trouble." Hugging me, she continued, "I can say no more, but ponder in your heart before you leave this wonderful, peaceful place that I have known since I was a child and you have grown to love."

The following day Aunt Hat called at midday. She came bearing a large handmade basket filled with sweets made the day before: jams, jellies, and a piece of goat cheese that pleased Granny to no end. Aunt Hat smiled as she carefully unwrapped the cheese, stating, "A gift from the Dusty People that I want to share with you."

The three of us had lunch outside. We ate Granny's homemade bread cut into large slabs, as she called them, spread with sweet cream butter that she churned that morning. Aunt Hat's wild berry jam topped the bread. I helped Granny with the buttermilk and sliced ham. A dish of fox grapes finished our meal, and we served sweets with our tea.

I knew Aunt Hat had something she wanted to say to me. Granny went about her usual chores, leaving the two of us to ourselves. I found myself wondering if birds carry messages between the two, or if thoughts flew about, received telepathically by one or the other.

"I have a book I have written. I was told I should place it in your hands when Granny is no longer with us, but I sense you will not be needing this," she stated softly. "I have recorded many important cures and health aids in these pages, treatments known to the mountain people, food from the forest that will sustain life in time of famine or disaster, and hundreds of things that are beneficial to mankind. Someone will follow in Granny's footsteps. She was so sure it would be you."

Aunt Hat sounded so sorrowful that I ran into the forest and cried. My heart was filled with sadness, and my days remaining in the mountains were few.

CHAPTER 31

My Last Walk With Granny

THE LAST TIME I walked with Granny, we went miles and miles deep into the high mountain forest. I felt the hurtful pain of breaking away. The leaves made a faint rustling sound as we stepped carefully among them, and I whispered a silent farewell to the majestic trees.

We reached the high meadow and stopped to catch our breath. I looked to the tall pine tree jetting out over the cliff. The eagle was no longer there, the nest was empty. We sank to the ground to rest. I picked up moss and cupped it in my hands to smell the clean, sweet smell of nature. I dug my fingers deep into the rich soil and allowed it to fall without a sound back into the floor of the forest.

We sat for fifteen or twenty minutes before rising and making our way back to the main trail. Suddenly Granny put her hand out to stop me, and we took time to listen. The forest was silent as death, not one sound could be heard. We waited with bated breath as the forest remained silent and time itself seemed to stand still. Then, suddenly, the many life sounds returned and I could hear the beautiful voice of the wind as it rushed through the trees and plants gracing this magnificent wooded area. Birds chirped nearby, a squirrel barked, and far away a fox called to its mate.

We both lifted our heads at the same time, wanting to hear more, waiting as the hum of life reached out to us. We were wrapped in the warm mountain air. We both knew this has been a special moment: the forest had given us a glimpse of its inner secrets, its understanding of our smallness, and allowed us to witness its greatness.

When it came time for me to leave, Granny gave me her egg money so I would have money for food for a while. That Monday morning we walked five miles to meet the mailman, who would take me to a town in North Carolina where I could take a bus or get a job, whatever I thought best for me. I carried my slippers and walked barefoot on the dusty road. My slippers were two sizes too large and they made blisters on my heels. People in the North Carolina mountains always bought large shoes for their children, as young feet would grow into them. They lasted longer and one didn't outgrow them so quickly.

Granny went with me the entire five miles, and then walked back home alone. She had prepared a little wicker basket of food, and we ate as we rested beneath a large tree that spread its branches out like an umbrella.

When we eventually arrived at the line of mailboxes, I went over to the creek and washed my feet in the cold water. I dried them with the sash Granny had made to match my dress. It was very wide, and when I tied it, it hung down the back to the hem. It was very wet when I finished, but I pressed it out over my knee and tied it back just as it was. Granny called the dress a pinafore. My straw hat was wide because of the sun's heat and it was very hard to keep on, so Granny gave me a hat pen she'd had for years and years. I loved it and have kept it with me always. It is still one of my most precious possessions.

The mailman arrived and I was installed in his car heading for Marshall, North Carolina, some seventy-five miles away. Granny had talked to me about not feeling afraid of anyone, but she had warned me to always be careful. She had given me her own pistol and I knew how to use it should the need ever arise.

PEARL K. MCCULLOUGH

CHAPTER 32

A New Beginning
At Thirteen Years Old

WHEN I ARRIVED in Marshall I went into the first shop I came across, which happened to be an eating place, and I purchased a large bottle of orange pop. While I was drinking this, an elderly man came in and sat down on the stool next to me. He asked the proprietor for a glass of hot water and a spoon. When he received this, he picked up a bottle of catsup from the lunch counter and poured most of it into the glass. After stirring it up, he drank most of it down without stopping.

I realized the man was hungry, but I disliked even sitting by him. Why I did it I will never know, but I told the proprietor to give this man some lunch and I would pay for it. He asked to see my money first, so I untied my handkerchief that had been tied in two knots. Granny had given it to me like this with the money in it. I paid fifty cents for the plate lunch that man ate, and I was left with eight dollars. I knew Granny had to sell a lot of eggs for that much money and I felt badly for having allowed her to give it to me.

Shortly afterwards the counterman asked if I knew how to serve food. He said his girl hadn't come in that day. I said, "Yes," but neglected to tell him the only food I had served was hay to the horses and cows, and a gift of leftovers to old Flossy, our dog; but I had been watching, and I thought I could do it.

I didn't have to write out the orders. When I got an order, I stopped at the window and delivered it verbally. The cook had to tell me three times to call out louder. After that it was, "I can hear you now."

I worked for about a week serving food and was just beginning to think it wasn't too bad when one day the counterman had to be away from the diner, and he told me I would be responsible for the money that day. I know my face showed my surprise. What he didn't know was that I wasn't sure how far I could count without Granny's hickory nuts! Well, sometimes I had two or three men waiting in line to go back to work, but they were nice, and I found I was able to make change after all. God surely helped me because no one had large bills that day, but the time could have played a big part in this, for the year was 1936.

I worked in the restaurant for two weeks, and then I was offered a job by a foreman who came to town looking for a cook for his logging camp. He told me the last man they had cooking for them got ill suddenly and that he had to take him home, and now the man refused to go back. He promised me a lot more money than what I was making at the diner. I needed the job, but I was afraid to go off into the mountain with only men, so I told him if he could find another woman to go along, I would take the job.

When he left the restaurant I didn't expect him to ever return, but the next day at noon he was back, telling me he had found a black man who wanted to work in the shed as a sawyer and his wife Mattie Lou had agreed to come along and help with the cooking.

CHAPTER 33

The Logging Camp

THE SUN WAS sinking low in the April sky when we all piled into his old truck and started off for the logging camp. I didn't know until later that his camp was in the mountains of Tennessee. The old truck plugged along and I found myself falling asleep on Mattie Lou's shoulder. We stopped for gas and coffee, and then drove on and on. I was bone tired and my legs had gotten stiff, and I asked if we could stop and walk around, but the driver was in a big hurry to return as quickly as possible to his lumber work.

Just before I fell asleep I heard Mattie Lou tell the man I was only a child, and he answered that I had told him I was eighteen years old and that I was taking on a woman's job, so I had a long walk back if I was unable to fulfill my obligations.

Before we left Marshall, North Carolina, I sold Granny's pistol and used my restaurant salary and my egg money of eight dollars to buy a .22 rifle. The first day of camp I didn't get much time to look around since when we arrived it was dusky dark, but the next morning with the first good light, I was out setting up can lids on the fence posts for my first target practice at the camp. I wanted all these rough men to know I could take care of myself. I was so sure that my ability would be tested, but I was wrong. I didn't have any trouble. I often think of those as the first kind men who entered my life.

On the way in for supper each evening, several of the men would bring in armloads of wood and stack it in the wood box. Their acts of kindness were not few.

Dried food was plentiful. I'm sure this food has been preserved in much the same manner as Granny had taught me. I made dried apple pies about three times a week. I cooked berries, which Mattie Lou picked, and used these for pies and jams. We made homemade bread every day and my arms ached up to my shoulders afterwards from all the dough kneading. Mattie Lou rubbed me with horse liniment to relieve the soreness.

The two of us hunted for wild greens on the hillsides and cooked them in a large iron pot with salt pork. Beans stood in water to soak on the back burner overnight, as they needed an early start the next morning. Sometimes there were shell beans and sometimes leather britches (leather britches are green beans that have been dried). We had homemade kraut in barrels, and corn pickled in brine, and finally, pickled beans.

Mattie Lou started a garden with seeds she found in a shed, and soon we had turnip greens, collards, and other good vegetables to grace the large table. That table was made from rough sawn timber with large benches on both sides and one wooden nail keg at each end. The foreman sat at one end and the shed boss at the other.

Mattie Lou and I cooked three meals a day for twenty-eight men. They used tin plates and cups, and spoons were placed on the table in a large glass so everyone could just help himself. Immediately after the meal, we washed the dishes and the table was reset for the next meal. Plates, cups and glasses were turned upside down to keep the flies and dust from them.

One of the men was a wood-carver, and he could carve a piece of twisted stick to look like a snake, a spider, or a lizard. We often found these on the floor of the shed, and Mattie Lou, unable to tell the difference between the real and the fake, was a great screamer, so she was at the mercy of these men. No harm was meant, I'm sure, but they sure liked to tease.

PEARL K. MCCULLOUGH

One day when Mattie Lou went for milk from the springhouse near the kitchen, she ran back screaming that a snake was in the springhouse. I grabbed my rifle and rushed out. It wasn't a snake at all, of course, just a carved, crooked stick placed there as a joke. But it wasn't a joke to Mattie Lou, poor thing; she nearly had a conniption fit! That night I made a large blackberry pie in a deep bread pan. When I placed the pie on the table after we had eaten dinner, everyone grabbed a spoon and waited to be served. Mattie Lou quickly disappeared, saying she absolutely refused to stay to see what was to happen, but I stood my ground. I tapped a glass for attention and told the men I wanted to say something. "Sirs, I know you like blackberry pie, and tonight you have something special. Mattie Lou ran into a friend of yours in the springhouse, and we invited him to dinner. You will find him in your pie."

I started to walk away, then added, "I forgot to tell you, we caught and used only the rat, the snake got away." Not one word was spoken. That was the first and last joke played on Mattie Lou. (Everyone knew that where there are snakes you'll also find rats because rats are a good source of food for the snakes. I had insinuated that we put a rat in the pie. This wasn't true, of course, but the men didn't know that. That pie stayed around for several days, and we finally had to throw it away.)

I stayed at the lumber camp for one season, a season lasting from six to nine months, from when a camp was set up 'till there was no more timber. During this season the camp moved twice in nine months, each time making a new campsite near a large stand of trees to be harvested for lumber. Mules and horses pulled the trees to the sawmill (mules, being more surefooted than horses, were used more often on the steep mountain slopes).

Mattie Lou and I should have been paid every month, the same as the men, but we weren't. When I asked about this, I was told each time, "Don't worry, you'll get paid before we leave the camp, we keep an account of this."

Every month I told them I was leaving, yet I stayed on, still believing some day I would get paid. But during this time I never received one red cent, and Mattie Lou's time was also for nothing. We decided we had been donating our time and labor to the wrong cause and made plans to leave as soon as we could because the camp would close come winter, and winter was getting nearer each day. We talked of walking out, but we both felt we would have a hard time getting down the mountain without being seen.

One day one of the men ran into camp very out of breath and said Buck, Mattie Lou's husband, had fallen and the new saw ripped him across his chest. The men thought he was dying. Mattie Lou screamed until I had to dash cold water in her face to hush her up.

I grabbed some clean cloths, a sack needle, some coarse thread, and a gallon of coal oil we used for lamps and to start fires, and followed the man back to the sawmill. I recall a potato was stuck on the spout of the oilcan to stop it leaking, and I pulled it off and threw it away but later wished I hadn't, as I spilled some of the oil when it sloshed from the can.

When we arrived at the camp, all the sawmill hands were gathered around Buck, who was stretched out on some boards. They parted and let me through the circle.

Mattie Lou took one look at her husband and started screaming again. That man was cut from his hip all the way to his collarbone. His eyes had rolled back into his head until all that was visible were the whites of his eyes. I pulled the wound open and could see that the deepest cut was in his stomach. His chest was ripped open but no bones were exposed.

Without thinking what to do next, I dropped the needle into the coal oil can and, holding one end of the thread, swished it around. Next I told the foreman to pour some oil on my hands, and I washed

PEARL K. MCCULLOUGH

them just as I'd seen Granny do. When I went over to Buck and picked some pieces of sawdust from the wound, I saw that about four or five inches of his intestines were oozing out of the cut. I worked as quickly as I could because I knew that his heavy breathing would push them out further if the opening wasn't closed. While the mill foreman poured oil on the wound, I sewed up that poor man, starting near his hipbone and going all the way up to his collarbone. I took a few extra stitches where the wound was deep.

Moving Buck back up the mountain took much longer and was harder than the mad rush down. The men fashioned a litter using two poles and the big saw covered by a tarpon, and four men took turns carrying the wounded man back to camp. I had them put Buck in my room and we covered him with blankets. Then we all went outside.

I got the lantern and had to almost drag Mattie Lou to help me, for I knew that not too far away there were herbs that would help Buck and perhaps save his life. In thirty minutes we had all we needed, and I showed Mattie Lou how to crush them, start them to fast cooking and then to simmering. She failed to wash the first batch, so we had to begin all over again. I remember thinking, "What's the difference, since the poor man probably already has two or three ounces of coal oil in his insides anyway."

We stayed up all night. There was no supper, but no one complained. We fed Buck hot herb tea as soon as it was ready. I put the spoon in his mouth and told him to swallow, and if he didn't, I stroked his throat until he did. I kept various hot medicinal leaves on his chest and stomach all night, changing them when they began to cool.

Buck's eyes were closed, and he seemed to be sleeping. His breathing became easier. I stood by his bed and looked at him, thinking that Granny was right when she said, "A man's days are few and full of trouble." I never closed my eyes that night. I rushed back and forth from the big kitchen to the small bedroom all night, constantly boiling more leaves for tea and for the herbal packets I packed on his chest.

In the early morning hours, just as the sun was rising, Buck opened his eyes and tried to look around the room. I spoke to him and told him not to move, that he had been hurt, and that he was in my bed. I reached for his hand and held it for a few minutes to let him know he wasn't alone. He closed his eyes, but each time I went to the kitchen for tea, when I returned, he opened them. He did not have a fever although I expected him to. When the men began to stir I told them he was awake, and I believed he would live. I also told them he needed a doctor and asked that they get one as soon as possible.

The men waited all day for things to change for the worse, but Buck held his own. One more trip was made to the woods, and this time not two but ten people went along, not to dig for herbs but to observe.

Days passed, and for a time I was afraid Buck might die after all. Most days I could hardly get to the stove for all the men crowded around; most of them were not working during this time, and everyone wanted to help. Eventually Buck asked for food, but somehow I felt he shouldn't eat yet. So I asked him if he would settle for a cup of herb tea instead. He said yes.

After almost a week the foreman asked me if I really thought Buck would live. "Sure," one man shot back. "If she didn't, she wouldn't have wasted all that thread!" I guess I must have established a good reputation in the camp along about then.

Shortly after that Buck was sitting up; in three weeks he was walking around outside. I remarked one day that it seemed strange the doctor hadn't come when he was told about the accident.

"It wasn't strange at all," one little guy said. "We were so busy watching a cricket hopping around, we forgot to go get him!" From that time on I was known as "Cricket" by one and all.

PEARL K. MCCULLOUGH

With the first heavy frost, we made ready to leave camp, and I was asked if I would come back in the spring to cook again. I told them this had been an experience I was unlikely ever to forget, but that no, I would not be returning next spring.

The second frost was much heavier and crisp, and so cold that we needed jackets. The third frost was a killing one, and we all agreed that we must leave as soon as possible before winter arrived with its chilling winds and blanket of snow that would cover everything for some time.

When winter arrived it brought many changes in the mountains. One awakened to a bright, new, white world with ice cycles hanging from the trees. Every leaf and piece of wood was covered with snow or a thin covering of ice, so cold but so beautiful. When the sun rose, the whole forest sparkled and twinkled as if chuckling to itself over hiding its secrets until spring.

The animals seemed impatient to go down the mountain. We had only a few more days and then we would move the whole camp, leaving only the saw, the empty sheds, and many memories behind us. The men were busy getting everything together as they wanted to leave straight away, and finally, no one was left in camp but Buck, Mattie Lou and me.

When a man from the lumber company came to pay the men and check over the camp, he stayed and talked for some time before leaving. When no one returned to camp and the evening was waning, he decided to leave because he had another camp to check. He left the men's pay with me, and I assured him they would get what they were entitled to.

As soon as he was out of sight I knew exactly what I intended doing. I believe Mattie Lou had similar thoughts, but she insisted all the way down the mountain that I had talked her into it. I put each white envelope on the table and picked it up several times, turning it over and thinking that part of this money was surely mine.

I was convinced that no one had the slightest intention of ever paying me. I should have received a dollar from each man each month. There were twenty-eight men so my pay would have amounted to $28 per man, and as I had worked for nine months, the total due me would have been $252. The same amount was due Mattie Lou, so I took it upon myself to pay us both from each man's pay envelope.

We took a horse for Buck to ride, and Mattie Lou and I walked down the mountain. The last time I saw them was in Slabtown, Tennessee near a crossroads, waving good-bye to me. We left the horse with a farmer to give to the logging men when they passed his farm. I never heard of Mattie Lou again, but years later, I met a lady with a fantastic story of a man she had met who told her a story of his accident in a sawmill. The lady who told me this story stated that he must have been telling the truth because she had seen the scar, and then she went on to describe it to me. I knew this man could have been no one else but Buck. There couldn't have been two scars like his!

PEARL K. MCCULLOUGH

CHAPTER 34

Next Stop,
Louisville, Kentucky

A T THE BUS station in Slabtown I was trying to decide where to go next when a man and woman sat next to me and we began to talk. They asked me where I was going, when my bus was leaving, and so on. I told them the first thing that popped into my mind—that I was going to Louisville, Kentucky. The man laughed and said that's where they were going. They were returning home after visiting his wife's sick mother. So I bought a ticket and took the same bus they did. What a blessing they turned out to be! When we arrived in Louisville, they took me into their home for several days, and even helped me to find a room with a nice motherly woman.

Every day I walked about the streets watching people and listening to them talk. When I went back to my room, I tried to remember what was said during my walks. For long hours, I practiced talking as they did in front of a mirror. I knew I was different both in my talk and dress, and I so wanted to learn to be like others. I desperately wanted to change this.

One day I walked into a shoe store and startled myself by saying, "Madam, I would like to purchase a pair of slippers, please." The lady showed me several pair of slippers before I made a choice, as I wanted to hear how one would talk to customers if by chance I ever sold shoes. Little did I know that the owner of this very shoe store would play a big part in my life!

I found a job in a tiny restaurant called The Bean Pot down the street from the shoe store. I worked long, hard hours. Not only did I serve food, but I also took it upon myself to clean the place from top to bottom. If I heard talk I thought to be intelligent, I stayed as near as possible and cleaned one spot over and over until it sparkled with cleanliness, while I eavesdropped. I listened mostly to shop workers who came in for lunch or coffee, and I learned so much by just doing my job and keeping my ears attuned that soon I felt more comfortable speaking and was no longer afraid of people asking me where I came from.

The shoe store owner came in each day to have lunch. He liked chili beans, and we had a Bean Pot specialty. I learned that he had never married. He was thirty-six years old and his name was Robert Seymour. This kind man came by late in the evenings and asked me to walk with him in a small park nearby. We sat and talked, and I knew he was just as lonely as I was. I found myself looking forward to our talks and our time together.

One day, the restaurant owner told me Robert had asked if he would mind if Robert asked me to work in his shoe store. I wanted to be honest with this kind man, so when he personally asked me to work for him, I told him my education was limited. Just how limited I did not reveal. He told me there wasn't one thing in the store he couldn't teach me if I made the effort. I was willing, and in six months I could handle everything, including helping him do inventory.

As time passed, I grew not only in height (I was always large for my age) but also in knowledge. I learned quickly and often startled myself by doing things that would have been impossible for me two or three months earlier.

There was a rough spot in the street just outside our door, and I found myself bandaging many cut knees for children and helping up older people who had fallen. Each time I thought, "I did this, my place is surely with sick people, or those who have no one, the same as me at one time."

One day, I plucked up my courage and spoke to Robert, telling him I was going home to see my father. I wanted to ask him to help me get into some type of school. I wanted to be a nurse, and I knew that without proper education I could never become one.

After much bolstering of my courage, I arrived at my father's house meek as a lamb, ready to talk with him about the early days of my childhood suffering, of the many sleepless nights when my pillow had been soaked with tears, of the rape, hate, and troubles that had filled my young heart to capacity.

I tried to show my father I loved him, and fell on my knees before him and begged him to please let me talk to him. All the while I tried to hug him close to my heart. Well, he almost knocked me over getting to his room!

That night, I heard him tell my oldest brother Edd that I should be put away where I wouldn't hurt anyone. He told Edd that I had always been feeble-minded. This was the last time I tried to communicate with my father.

Robert had told me he had a sister in nearby St. Charles, Virginia, and if I ever needed to talk to him, I could get in touch through her. She was the owner of Bea's Beauty Shop. I went to see her, and she said Robert had told her of me and to call him if I needed help. She called him while I was there, and the next day he knocked on my father's door and asked to see me. He told my sister, Mary, I had worked for him in his shoe store, and that while visiting his sister he thought he'd look me up.

Mary and I had never really gotten along, and she did not believe this for one moment and went to find my father at once. In the meantime I pulled Robert out on the porch and asked him to take me somewhere so we could talk. He took me back to his sister's, and we talked for hours. I fell on my knees before this kind, gentle man, and opened my heart, pouring out all the hatred, pain, and sorrow, and telling of the agonizing years that had passed since my eighth birthday.

Robert didn't say a word while I was talking, but when I had finished, he dried my eyes and lifted me to an upright position. Putting his arms around my shoulders, he asked if I would be willing to marry him, and in this way perhaps he could help me. He was dismayed when I told him I was only fourteen years old. He wanted to talk to my father, but I knew if this happened, it would mean the end to everything.

So Robert and I went to Cumberland Gap in Tennessee, not too far from Middlesborough, Kentucky, and there we were married by a justice of the peace. I told the justice I was eighteen years old and he did not question me.

We spent two weeks together in a little mountain cottage that we rented, talking and making plans for our life together. The consummation of our marriage never occurred, as Robert told me that when I wanted to give myself to him completely, with love and without fear, we would both know. He would wait because my happiness and the trust I had given him meant more than words. "Don't tell me you love me until you really do. And when that time comes, words will be unnecessary. I will know, but more important, you will know."

After two weeks, we went back to my father's home for my clothes and to talk with him. This was not my idea. Had it been left to me, I'd never have returned at all.

My father asked to speak with me alone, but I refused unless Robert was beside me. He then asked to speak with Robert alone and they went into the living room and closed the door. I stood in the hallway and listened to my father's loud voice for such a long time. I heard him say he could have our marriage annulled since I was only fourteen years old. Robert's soft voice answered my father by saying, "If you care, you could see that she is a frightened, unhappy girl and needs love and care more than anyone I have ever met."

My father then went on to tell Robert of my "mental illness", how the doctor had told him years ago that I was a danger to others and myself. He told him things I supposedly had told Mary, my sister, things I knew nothing of, terrible things my mind could never have conceived of.

When Robert came out of the room I felt he was looking at me as if seeing me for the first time. "Katherine, I want you to make up your mind what is best for you. Don't do anything for a few days. I will be leaving for Louisville on Sunday."

I was devastated! It appeared to me that Robert had believed every lie my father had told him about me and that he was deserting me, leaving me to whatever fate my father might have in store for me.

That night I lay wide awake, but with no tears. My tears had dried, and I felt that the pieces of my life lay shattered at my feet. My feelings of desertion had turned to a storm of anger, and I wanted to create a wind that would scatter them, my family and Robert as well, in all directions.

The next morning, I rose from my bed and began a plan of action that shook the neighborhood for days. First, in revenge for Mary's lies, I cut up most of her clothes into strips and left them strewn over the room. She had so much, and I had so little, and as we'd never gotten along I had no qualms about getting back at her.

Next, I traveled several miles to a place called Walnut Park in Pennington Gap, Virginia, and rented a room. As soon as it was dark, I went into a café and picked up the first man I spoke to and took him to my room. There, I gave myself to him, hating myself and hating him even more. *If you have the name, play the game*, I kept telling myself. My father wanted a feeble-minded daughter, and I intended to see that he had a feeble-minded daughter! Once the man was asleep, I took his clothes, wallet, and everything he had. The next morning they were placed on his wife's porch, with a signed note from me telling what had happened.

Not one, but five such notes were found in that community in one week. I gave them my name, my father's name, and my age. In each note I said that the man had not taken advantage of me, but rather that I had taken advantage of him. This was not only to clear him in his wife's eyes, but also was my way of getting back at my father.

News like this traveled quickly in a small town such as the one in which my father lived. On advice of his attorney, my father started annulment proceedings of my marriage, but then stopped the proceedings, again on the advice of his attorney once he heard Robert was divorcing me on grounds of adultery. Upon learning that, my father wanted nothing more to do with me.

Two years later, Robert did sue me for divorce, and the divorce was granted since I did not appear in court. How could I, being guilty and with five men probably willing to testify as to my actions during the week in the Walnut Park Hotel apartment?

Robert's sister, Bea, came to see me and told me he had waited for me at her home until Sunday before going back to Louisville, believing I would clear myself of my father's claim of feeble-mindedness and confinement in an institution and come to him.

I told Bea I had thought Robert deserted me, and she forgave me for involving her brother along with the other five men involved in the scandal, although she went to court on her brother's behalf later. I thought she understood I was lashing out at my father and, in fact, all men. The day we talked, she told me she could not hate me and neither did her brother, but that he was very hurt. She tried to embrace me, but I pulled away and walked out of the room. What made all this even sadder was that unbeknownst to me, one of the five men I "seduced" was Bea's own husband!

PEARL K. MCCULLOUGH

I spent the days following this scandal at home in a locked room, and no one was allowed to talk to me. Meanwhile I was making plans to run away as soon as I had a chance. I still had some of the money I had earned working at the shoe store, and I knew that one day I would be able to walk out of that room and keep walking away as far as possible.

When an opportunity finally presented itself to leave, I walked six miles and waited at the fork in the road until dawn. One road was going off in the direction of Harlan, Kentucky. When a truck slowed down, the driver asked me where I was going. I told him, "Just anywhere." He opened the door and I got in. He asked my name, then turned the truck around and took me straight home to my father. Unfortunately for me, he knew my father.

That was the first time my father laid a hand on me. He beat me with a wide belt he used to sharpen his razor with. My back and arms were bruised and bleeding. I did not cry out, I stood silent while all this happened. When he had exhausted himself, he asked me, "Now, what is your next plan?" I told him he had better beat me to death because I fully intended to kill him. He threw the belt down and walked out of the room. I picked up my suitcase and followed him. He did not try to stop me this time.

I walked back to the crossroads in St. Charles, and there I again waited for a ride to Harlan, Kentucky. When a truck stopped and before I got in, I told the driver my name and my father's name, and showed him my back and arms. Then I said, "Now, if you want to be responsible for a murder, go ahead take me back because that is what I intend to do if he ever raises a hand to me again."

The man had me walk across the state line from Virginia to Kentucky (right there at the crossroads), and then I got into the truck and rode it into Harlan.

CHAPTER 35

"Bloody Harlan," Kentucky

HARLAN, KENTUCKY, WAS known as "Bloody Harlan". Several coalmines were located there. The men were rough and there was much violence in the streets. This town was open to anything. I was frightened within an inch of my life because I had heard of this place. Wherever I looked, I saw defeat.

But I could not go home. I had no place to go, I was alone and was certain beyond a doubt that death awaited me somewhere, and I believed with all my heart I was seeking it. I did not care what happened to me. I just wanted to get it over with. I was not the only girl in this situation, there were many others.

I had to eat, so I looked for a restaurant. The truck driver had warned me to be off the streets early and not to "go over the bridge". It seems the bridge was a dividing line between the more decent and the bad parts of Harlan. Truthfully, I don't think there was any part of Harlan but the bad part. The four months I was there, I saw things many people would not believe. I learned that our world is what we make for ourselves, and it can often be a jungle. Only those who have been in that jungle would understand.

While eating, I talked with the waitress and she told me two girls had been killed the night before. She gave me all the details. One girl was found choked to death and the other had been pushed from a window. I laughed and told her it was a pity it couldn't have been me, and she replied, "Now honey, don't be so tough on yourself. The whole world is not mad at you, is it?"

A police officer came into the café for coffee, and he asked me if I was a stranger in town. I told him, "Yes, and I need to find a job." He offered to take me the next day to see a lady who needed help. I agreed to meet him at the restaurant.

After he left the waitress wanted to know what he was talking to me about, and I told her he was going to help me get a job.

"Kid, he'll just take you to Jewel's, that's the second place across the bridge. Why don't you just walk over and present yourself? You'll save yourself $250. That's what Slim gets for each girl he takes to Jewel's. Jewel takes it out of your pay at so much a week until it's paid off."

I was shocked that a policeman would do such a thing and I told her so, but she told me if I stayed in Harlan long enough, nothing would shock me.

I left the café before dark to find a room. I had a hot bath, and started thinking. I thought about Granny. She would be having her dinner just about this time, the chores all done. I could close my eyes and almost see her working on her quilt, mending, or deep in thought with hands together, as if praying. *Oh, Granny, Granny! Why have all these things happened to me?* I began thinking perhaps I should go back to her and the mountains. I could live and die there, just as Granny was doing. She was a part of the mountains and the mountains a part of Granny. They were inseparable.

I couldn't sleep and went to the window and watched people on the street most of the night. What a nightmare one can have without sleeping! There are nightmares that go on and on, and you realize that sleep flies from you at a time like this. That night I relived my life from the time I was eight years old. I wanted to cry, but my eyes remained dry and my heart felt like a lump of lead in my breast.

I fell asleep in the chair and awakened the next morning to a knock on my door. It was the landlady; she invited me to have breakfast with her. I cleaned my room and walked downstairs. She was a lovely lady; she talked to me while we ate. I told her I had run away from home and she begged me to go back. She offered to call my family. She told me I couldn't be in a worse place, but I insisted I could take care of myself.

I boarded with this lady for only one week. I knew I must get a job, but it seemed the only work to be found was in a restaurant or a honky-tonk. I got a job in the Blue Ribbon, a honky-tonk.

I told the manager I had worked in places like this before, and he gave me some rules that must be obeyed: (1) Mingle with everyone and don't stay with one guy all evening; (2) Get men to play the juke box, dance, and buy drinks; The girls' drinks were made from something that had no liquor in it; (3) We were never to leave the building with a man; (4) Our job was to see that the customers spent their money there. The more they spent, the bigger our cut was. We got a percentage on every drink sold, and they paid for our drinks too, paid for whiskey although we were drinking colored water.

Sometimes we danced all night and slept all day the following day, then started the same routine all over again. I still wasn't fifteen years old, but I passed easily for eighteen.

I'd worked at the honky-tonk for about six weeks when one of the other girls and I went shopping for some clothes. While in the store I put my bag down to look at a dress, and when I turned around, my bag was going out the door on the arm of a girl no older than myself. I ran behind her for about half a block and stopped her. She handed the bag over without a word.

The owner of the store and a policeman were there by that time. The girl turned to me, and she had the same hopeless look in her eyes I had seen in so many other helpless people. I put my arms around her and told the officer I had made a mistake, she wasn't taking my bag.

I took her back to the Blue Ribbon with me, and that night she told me she was pregnant. She was sixteen years old, and she'd been

PEARL K. MCCULLOUGH

a prostitute since she was thirteen. I wept with her as she gave me all the details of her life. She had worked over the bridge, but when she became pregnant Madam Flo told her she had to leave. She wasn't even allowed to take her clothes. She had no money, and she took my purse because she hadn't eaten in two days, and she was desperate.

The next day Ruby showed me where Flo's place was, and Madam Flo had an angry, early morning caller. Flo was a large blonde lady with the most beautiful eyes I have ever looked into. We talked for about an hour. All this time I had the feeling that Flo and I understood each other; that we connected on some level.

I left there with Ruby's clothes, four boxes of beautiful wearing apparel, and $200 in cash. The cab driver charged me $10 fare for picking up these things, so I sent him back to Flo to collect, and she paid it. I was to see Flo again before I left Harlan.

I took Ruby to the landlady where I had spent my first night, who rented her a room. Ruby couldn't even work at the Blue Ribbon because when she wore a dress that fit, one could tell she was already in her fifth month.

Ruby sold me all her clothes for $30, and I tried them all on, paraded around the room, and then hung them in my closet, never to wear them. I don't know why, but I just couldn't.

I wouldn't let Ruby spend one cent of her money. I paid her rent and bought her food. I knew she would need her money when the baby came, so we tucked it away for later. I spent most of my days with Ruby, even if I danced all night. I was fresh after just a few hours' sleep.

One day, Ruby wanted to stop on the street and listen to a man speaking. He was a minister, and we stopped and listened for about fifteen minutes. Ruby started crying, and I pulled her away and we went home. The next day she wanted to talk about the minister and how guilty she felt about how she'd been living, about how hard her life had been, and how she'd gotten into prostitution. She believed in the hereafter and wanted to talk about that, but I refused to listen. After that I wouldn't go near that street corner when we were together. I had enough problems already without my conscience going on a rampage.

Ruby began to talk to me about her family, and little by little she pulled me from my own shell. I told her about Granny and my years on the mountain. When we talked of my father, I cried and could not stop, and she hugged me and insisted that something good would happen if I could stop hating and allow it to. She wanted me to stop working at the Blue Ribbon.

She said, "Most girls who work there eventually end up at Flo's or Jewel's place. You are not that type, please stop and do something else. Those girls are hard as nails."

"Something like what?" I asked. "Work in the mines?"

One day, the landlady ran out to meet me and told me Ruby was ill. She had been trying to get a doctor, but to no avail. When I asked Ruby who her doctor was, she said she had not seen a doctor. I could tell she was very sick because she looked so pale and weak. I left the house to find someone to help. I called three doctors, and when I told them of Ruby's condition, their advice was to get her to a hospital. They would not come, giving as an excuse that she needed hospital care.

When I ran back up the street, I saw a group of people and I realized they were gathered around the minister whom I had avoided like the plague. I went to him and pulled him aside, telling him that a lady was very ill and needed help. He responded at once, and in less than ten minutes we were climbing the stairs to Ruby's room.

Rev. Richard Scole spoke softly to Ruby, telling her she would be going to the hospital as soon as the ambulance arrived. I heard him using the hall phone to call the ambulance, still speaking in a soft, gentle tone of voice. He then alerted the hospital. When the ambulance arrived, he didn't ask if I wanted to go along, he took my arm and guided me into one of the seats in the back, so I could be with Ruby. He sat on the other seat and held her hand.

I watched as he lowered his head, and I knew he was praying. When we arrived at the hospital, it was obvious that everyone knew he was a minister. They greeted him warmly, and one could see the staff respected him.

I went to the waiting room and sat for hours. Rev. Scole came in to see if I knew any of Ruby's family or where they could be located. I told him she had spoken of a family but had never given me any names or addresses. I told him she had worked at Flo's place, and that Flo might know something of the family.

He walked out, returning shortly with the information that Flo said she knew nothing whatever about this girl.

This man rarely left the hospital for a day and a night, and I did not leave at all. I couldn't. I sat as if glued to my chair. I wanted to be near Ruby, even though I was unable to help her. When Rev. Scole came into the waiting room with a nurse, I knew before he said one word that Ruby was dead. He told me she was conscious for only two hours after being admitted to the hospital, and then she had slipped into unconsciousness and remained so until she died.

Rev. Scole accompanied me to Ruby's room, while I took care of her few belongings. Then I told him I was going to the Blue Ribbon to get my things. I would stay in Ruby's room for a few days. He insisted on going with me and helped me pack my things in boxes. I had only one small suitcase. He later told me he was afraid if I went alone, I would be talked into staying.

When at last I went to sleep, I dreamed of that night in the mountains when I walked into a woman's world and left my childhood behind me. I awakened, weeping, and continued to weep not for the child that was never to be, but for the children that would be brought into a world unloved and unwanted, the victims of circumstance. How I wished I could see Granny and let her hold me. I knew I would find comfort in her arms and strength in her wisdom.

The funeral plans, made by the minister and paid for by the county, were completed, and Ruby's remains were laid to rest on a bleak, cold rainy day in a cemetery on a hillside in Hagan, Kentucky, five miles from Harlan. I asked Rev. Scole to hold a service, as I felt Ruby would want this. I liked what he said: "Lord, this young lady's path has just crossed mine. I don't know much about her, but Lord, you know of her suffering and her sorrow. She is one of Your children. You say in Your word, 'Come unto me you that are weary and heavy laden and I will give you rest. I now commit Ruby to You.' Amen."

I packed my clothes and burned all the things of Ruby's that I got from Flo. Then I went to see Rev. Scole and met his beautiful wife. I told them I was leaving the next day. They had wanted me to stay and help them with their ministry, but I could not. When he walked to the door with me, Rev. Scole gave me some good advice: "Katherine, you are running away from something. You had better turn around right now and face it, for whatever it is will follow you until you do." I wish I knew where to find him now, so I could tell him he was right.

I felt for some reason I should visit Flo's place once more before leaving Harlan behind me. As I started to cross the bridge, the wind was blowing so hard that I walked slowly, holding onto the side rail. Several pieces of paper had been blown into the water, and I watched as they slowly turned in tiny whirlpools as if on a spindle until they passed out of sight.

When I arrived at the large house and climbed the stairs, I knew Flo had heard of Ruby's death. She invited me in, and we talked for some time. I met all the girls that day, and I told Flo that I had a lot to thank Ruby for. The day Ruby took my purse I had made up my mind I was going to Flo's or Jewel's to ask for a job. I was looking for

PEARL K. MCCULLOUGH

new clothes when we met. What that girl saved me from she will never know. I have so often wondered if our paths crossed for two reasons: one, to give Ruby a friend when she needed one so desperately, and two, for me to be saved from a fate worse than death. One of the girls walked back over the bridge with me so I wouldn't be alone. I looked back to see her looking down at the water with her head bent low.

CHAPTER 36

A Move to Lexington, Kentucky, and Thoughts of a Better Life

M Y NEXT STOP was Lexington, Kentucky. I was fifteen years old at this time. While in Harlan I had met a man who told me at the time he was wealthy, but I did not believe it. He had given me his telephone number and address, and I had promised to look him up when I left Harlan.

When I called him, I had money but was mad at the world, so I hitchhiked to Bowling Green, Kentucky, where we were to meet at a horse show. This was on a Friday and I arrived late, having gotten a ride with a cattleman. My suitcase was hung on a peg on the back of his truck cab. You can imagine what this looked like, after riding with five cows that had just been taken off green grass pasture.

My friend was there, as he had promised. Two things he insisted on: one, that he pay the cattleman for my ride, and two, that he throw my suitcase, boxes, and everything else I had, away.

I rode to Kentucky with Sam and his chauffeur, and we spent that night in the caretaker's house on the north grounds of his palatial mansion. The next day, one of the stable boys came by with a message for him, and he left to take care of business affairs. When he returned he took me to town to the city's nicest store. Here he selected and purchased for me the kind of clothes I had never been able to afford (or need)—riding habits, boots, gloves and evening gowns, even down to a custom-made silver-studded saddle!

Sam's wife was in Europe. I could lie here and say I spent five or six happy months with this man being babied and cared for. Truthfully, though, I had never been so miserable in my life! I realized I was doing wrong, and I couldn't look at myself in the mirror without feeling guilt-ridden. Thank God for one of Sam's horses that was to bring all of this to a screeching halt.

I had started seeing the other side of this man I was with every day. Sam drank morning, noon and night. His gentle, kind, and loving ways seemed only for his horses and for me. He was curt with the stable boys, often rude to his friends and associates, but never with me. He never corrected nor struck me, but I was afraid this could change at any moment.

I'd told Sam my age and he was stunned, and in fact didn't believe me at first. Meanwhile my dreams at night were getting so bad I couldn't sleep. I relived the scene in the barn loft when I was raped. I could see the man's face so clearly in my dream. Frequently I awoke screaming, flinging myself from the bed. I found it difficult to eat and I lost weight. Sam was concerned about my age and my health. He took me to his doctor who gave me a sleeping medication that didn't help the dreams and actually made things much worse.

Sam was the proud owner of one of the finest broodmares in the south. This mare was in foal, and on the night she was to drop her colt, several things happened that were to have an effect upon not only the mare and her offspring, which later developed into a champion, but also to two people whose destiny was linked to this occasion.

The mare was down when Sam came to the caretaker's house and asked me to come back to the stables with him. I sat on the stable floor and held the mare's head and tried to keep her from flinging herself about. It seems the foal was trying to be born backwards and this was causing many problems.

I talked to the mare and stroked her neck, and the stable boy brought me a bucket of water and I continued washing her face and stroking her left shoulder as she lay on her right side. It seemed that her eyes were filled with tears and rolled down her face.

Sam's veterinarian was nice and had much feeling for animals. He likewise sensed the mare's suffering. He was trying to turn the colt, and Sam was getting more excited as every moment passed. He was afraid Dr. Kenard would break the colt's neck. We all breathed a sigh of relief when the colt's head finally appeared. The stable boy began to rub the colt with a warm cloth when it was fully exposed, and the colt began to whinny.

The mare tried to get up and I stepped back so the men could help her. While they were trying to get her up, she started to stumble, and one of the stable boys grabbed her tail and twisted it to help get her to her feet. She screamed with pain but was unable to rise, and lay quivering.

Sam went into such a rage I couldn't look at him. He struck the stable boy twice with his fist before I could get between them. When he grabbed the braided leather lead from the stable boy, I cried out and held on to his arm. I had seen the strongest animal brought to its knees with one of these instruments of torture, a heavily braided line with barbs woven into the leather. It was wrapped around a horse's nose to keep it quiet if it was excited or was being "gingered." (Gingering is a term meaning to apply a paste made of ginger root to a horse's anus. The burning heat from the paste causes the horse to hold its tail very high, something people liked to see in show horses. It makes the horse look very pretty until you realize why the horse holds its tail that way.)

The rage in Sam's eyes was not to be ignored. In trying to get to the stable boy, Sam struck me on the neck and I fell against the stable gate.

When the roof stopped spinning, Dr. Kenard was washing my face with the cloth from the bucket I'd washed the mare's face with.

He told me Sam thought he had killed me and had gone to call the police.

After sending a boy to find Sam and let him know I was all right, I made my way cautiously to the caretaker's house and started getting my things together. When I had most of them piled high on the bed, I thought, "What the heck?" I threw them into the fireplace and left, wearing the riding habit Sam had selected for me.

The veterinarian was just pulling out of the drive, and I stopped his truck and climbed in beside him. We stopped at a small café and drank coffee and talked. He was understanding and had a listening ear. He let me do most of the talking, and I felt better. I talked mostly of Sam, our life together the last few months, and tonight's events. Dr. Kenard took me to the bus station where, as before, I left the mixed pieces of my life behind me, not wanting to look back, and closing my mind to what lay ahead.

CHAPTER 37

Augusta and Atlanta, Georgia; Blues in the Night

I N AUGUSTA, GEORGIA, I was ill, and when I found I was to be hospitalized, I gave them Katherine Tingley as my name and Sam's name as next of kin. He came as soon as possible and tried in every way to help me. He pretended I was his daughter, and no one, with the exception of the doctor, knew otherwise.

I was under treatment there for several months. The doctor gave me a shock treatment and would have given me more had not Sam objected. He knew that some people had undergone lapses of memory due to shock therapy, and they never recovered. He thought his action in the stable that night had been the cause of my anxiety. He was such an amiable gentleman when sober, absolutely impeccably mannered. However, when drinking, as he was the night the colt was born, he was a most disagreeable and insulting piece of humanity.

We stayed in Augusta for some time, and Sam's wife sued for divorce upon his return to Lexington.

Again I ran away from all these problems, including Sam, and I continued to run for a long time. I collapsed under the extreme strain of guilt and called for Sam's help several times. As always, he would rescue me, or so he thought.

I was allowed to almost destroy not only myself but others as well before I finally let God help me. I hurt this man who would have given anything to make me happy. He thought nothing was too good for me, and he always tried to show kindness, if not love. I really don't believe Sam loved anyone; he, like me, was incapable of loving or being loved. I closed this chapter of my life, feeling pity for anyone who came into contact with either of us as we were then.

My next job, when I was almost sixteen, was singing in a small, smoke-filled club near Atlanta, Georgia. One night when I was feeling especially low and desiring companionship, I made the acquaintance of a group of musicians who, a few days later, needed a female vocalist. After several nights of practice, they accepted me into their group. I auditioned with them, and we were hired on a two-week trial basis.

We played at seven different clubs after that. Most of the songs I was required to sing were sad, and some brought back memories of my childhood, particularly my time in the mountains with Granny. Even sad melodies without lyrics could produce tears at this difficult time in my life (I was then sixteen). Most of the songs were sad ballads or blues that brought back memories of difficult times in my own life. I was trying to forget the past, but I couldn't cope with all the noise in the smoke-filled halls where we played, or the people of every description, always loud and demanding. It felt to me like the whole world was laughing and I was the only one with anything to cry about. So I painted a smile on my face and sealed my emotions, or so I thought.

Soon the bandleader and I had a difference of opinion concerning the tears in my eyes rather than in my voice. I was supposed to be a "blues" singer. He could never understand why I cried when I sang. I talked to him about this, but I could never convey to him my feelings on this subject and we parted, though as friends. So ended my short-lived career as a singer! It turned out this was the very beginning for him of a successful career with the Grand Ole Opry in Nashville, Tennessee.

CHAPTER 38

Kindness and Encouragement Lead Me to South Carolina

I BOUGHT A bus ticket to Spartanburg, South Carolina, and as soon as I arrived, I asked the ticket agent if he knew of a nice boarding house. He called a lady he knew, Mrs. Sligh, who came down to meet me.

She rented me a nice room, and with time on my hands, I found things to do around the house. Without being asked I cleaned the house, often helped cook, and mended everything I could find that needed the attention of a needle and thread. I cleaned my room from top to bottom, and every drawer was dusted and put in order. I washed and ironed the frilly curtains and even cleaned the windows. I guess I made quite an impression on Mrs. Sligh, as she didn't want me to go out and get a job. She told me she wanted me to just rest and give myself time to find the right job. I was then sixteen, but she believed I was eighteen years of age, and that I had decided not to stay in the mountains, as this is what I told her.

I enjoyed the boarding house, and the boarders were nice and very friendly. A lovely lady lived there who taught school, and she tried several times to talk to me, but I always found an excuse to leave the room. I liked her, but I was afraid she would start asking questions of me.

I spent Christmas at Mrs. Sligh's, and on New Year's Eve, her sister and her husband from Augusta, Georgia, drove up to spend a few days. When it was time for them to return, they asked me to go with them and stay for as long as I wished. They even offered to help me get a job.

Mrs. Thompson also took me to meet the people she worked with. Soon I was at home in the office where she worked as a social worker for the county. I went on calls with her, and some days we spent the entire day "out in the field" as she called it. I loved this couple and I respected them. They were good to me, and I did everything I could to make our association a pleasant one. I worked with Mrs. Thompson for several months without pay in order to learn something of her work. Her concern for people was genuine.

I had worked there for about a year when I met a man, Ernest Collins, and in two weeks I married him. He was twenty-four years older than I was and he worked at the textile plant. I spent one night with him, and I left him before daylight, never to see him again. He was a very harsh man, and I realized I'd made a big mistake and had jumped into this marriage too quickly. We had gone to South Carolina to get married, as that's where his family lived. I couldn't get a divorce in South Carolina, so I went back to Georgia and had my marriage annulled there.

I next got a job selling cosmetics for Walgreen's Drug Store, where I received a salary plus a commission on sales. I was about seventeen years old at that time. I knew Jim Mason, the man in charge of these stores, liked me, and I did nothing to discourage him. Soon we were meeting for dinner, going out of town on trips, and in six weeks I had an apartment. He paid for a car, and I became his mistress.

Jim often told me he loved me, and although it wasn't true, I told him I loved him as well. I wanted a home and security, and this he gave me in exchange for my self-respect. I didn't like what I was doing and knew it was wrong, but I felt that no one cared. Jim never knew about my past life, and I didn't think it was necessary to tell him. He never asked questions and I didn't volunteer any information.

One week as he started to leave, Jim told me he was going to ask his wife for a divorce so he could marry me. I tried to make him see what he would be giving up because he had a wife and family, but he kept telling me he would call me later in the week and let me know what she said.

I was so terrified that night that I couldn't sleep. I knew that I didn't want to marry him; I had been using him for my own convenience. I felt guilty and ashamed that I would go this far with a man and not have any feelings for him other than self-preservation. I packed my bags, withdrew all the money I had from my account, and drove my car to Greenwood, South Carolina, where I stayed for six months.

Jim found me there, and I told him I didn't care for him. He was angry with me, but later said he deserved what he had gotten for treating his wife in such a manner. He had not asked her for a divorce after all, and much later I received a letter from him telling me they were happier than he had expected them to be. I never heard from him again.

PEARL K. MCCULLOUGH

CHAPTER 39

Working for the Textile Company

WHEN I ARRIVED in Greenwood I met a lovely girl about my own age. She introduced herself as Connie and told me she worked at the textile mill. We lived at the same boarding house where five other people rented from the owner. We talked often. My money from my previous job was disappearing fast and I knew I must find work, so Connie suggested I go with her and meet her boss.

I met Connie at the gate of the large gray textile plant and she took me inside to meet Mr. Powell. He seemed very nice and asked me if I would like to take what he described as a "sight test", saying he needed a cloth examiner. If I passed the test, I could start work the next day. I found myself seated before a big machine with a large roll of cloth passing before me. I learned to stop the machine, mark the bad oil spots in the cloth with soap that was removed later, and then restart the machine for further examination. In one week I was meeting the production quota, which meant I was examining thousands of yards of cloth per shift to keep the production at a required standard.

Not long after I started work, I was asked to come to the office where I talked with a person referred to as a "minute-man". He asked me if I would like to be a trainer and supervise other cloth examiners. I agreed to try, and the pay was a little better. Some of the women who had been there for years did not like me because of this promotion, and because the company was pushing them to produce more yardage per shift, stating they were low performers. I suggested more lighting be placed behind the cloth for better visibility, and production doubled in two years, but our salaries remained the same. For most of us, our salary was $23 a week, though most of the men made more.

Pressure was building toward unionizing the mill. I was asked several times to help, but I did not wish to become involved. Since childhood I had no respect for the unions, doubtless because of memories of my father's union involvement. However, I did not go to our supervisor and report any of this union activity. I think the people involved wanted to see if I would report them. When I didn't, I think they respected me more and made an effort to show me how they felt.

I became friendly with so many of the people in that area and liked them so well that I decided to stay. One day Mr. Powell, the man I worked for, introduced me to a friend of his, Mr. Douglas Crouch, who owned land in Greenwood County. Shortly after that meeting, Mr. Powell and Mr. Crouch left to visit Mr. Crouch's place in the country and Mr. Crouch told me if I wished to come along, I would be welcome. They picked me up at the boarding house and we drove out to his place.

The farmhouse sat on four hundred twenty-eight acres. It was a large structure set back behind trees, and had a horseshoe-shaped drive. For some reason I was very taken with this house. It seemed to represent something I'd been searching for without even realizing it. It wasn't beautiful, but I was certain that a woman's touch, hard work, and loving care could make this a place of indescribable beauty.

Mr. Crouch was unaware that because of his house and the land, I had already made up my mind to marry him.

CHAPTER 40

Desire and Disaster

SEVERAL DAYS LATER when we walked over some of his land, and then rode for hours on horseback, I acted shy and very aloof, and when he tried to hold my hand I quickly withdrew it and looked down as if shocked. I did not even let Douglas kiss me until we were married. I played my cards so well that even I was amazed at my own acting.

Eight months from the day we met, Douglas Crouch and I were married in Ware Shoals, South Carolina. I told Douglas I had no family, and since I had no intention of going home again, I felt I was safe. So after the marriage ceremony we went home to face his sister, Ruth, who was against the marriage in the first place, and so our life together began. I was then nineteen years old.

I loved living in the country, the quiet evenings at home and the warm nights when all you needed was a sheet covering you. The full moon rose and the mocking birds sang just outside our bedroom window, and the fragrance of jasmine and magnolia drifted into our room. My love of nature was a real asset during the years I lived in South Carolina. I did so much with the grounds and gardens. I lavished all the love within me on my surroundings that I was unable to share with those around me. I had a horse, and wouldn't permit her to be groomed unless I was nearby, and most of the time I tended to her myself.

There were several families living on our property as tenants, all of whom were black. Josephine was a favorite friend, and how she loved me and tried to protect me! She helped me to care for the house and eventually everything was placed in her gentle and loving hands, including our three lovely children, who arrived about eighteen months apart. Josephine loved her work and we loved her. She was a jewel and deserved much more than she received from our household.

When we first became husband and wife, Douglas was kind and gentle. However, that seemed to change when our first daughter was born. He seemed to harbor much resentment that she was not a boy. He mistreated me and then wanted to make love to me after each beating, always telling me that I caused him to do this by making him angry or disobeying him. I never knew what to do to please him. I came to dread the times we were together and became consumed more and more not only with fear but hatred as well.

In three years' time I learned that Douglas was cheating his loyal and trusting sharecroppers. What he took from them was more than I could repay, but I tried to see through manipulating the books that the damage was less than what it would have been had I not interfered. I always took Josephine into my confidence, and she always gave me the same advice: "Don't worry, and don't get too smart. Play dumb and you'll live longer!"

I disagreed, however, and continued tampering with Douglas' books. In so doing, I discovered that this wasn't just a one-year occurrence but that he had been taking advantage of these hardworking people for many years! I was filled with disgust, and finally confronted him with this evidence. He struck me several times with his open hand, and then, when I fought back, he dragged me into the harness room in the barn and tied my hands with a piece of leather. He gave me the worst beating a person can endure and still remain conscious. Josephine heard my screaming and begged my husband to stop. He finally did stop, but only after I promised never to go near his desk again, a promise I kept.

I had learned that Douglas' sister, Ruth, was a victim just as I was. Douglas often beat her if she showed the slightest rebellious nature, which we both seemed to have. We both feared for our lives, and we lived in terror of what my husband might do to us.

Ruth ran away when my daughter was two, and she never lived in South Carolina again. She died in a mental hospital years later. So I was alone with this person who was more beast than man.

About eighteen months from the birth of Melba Ruth, our first daughter, Sandra Sue, our second daughter was born, and in another eighteen months, a third daughter, Toby Elaine arrived. I named her after my husband's father, Toby Wellington Bono Crouch, just as he had requested or rather demanded the first time he saw her.

CHAPTER 41

Dr. Bill

THE NIGHT I was beaten so badly, I had to be taken to see a doctor. Douglas told Dr. Bill I had fallen from a sled and injured myself. I also told the same story because that was what I was told to say. Dr. Bill did not believe our statements and told us so, and I was sent home with Douglas that night.

The next day I became ill and was admitted to the hospital in Greenwood, South Carolina. I did not know then that I was pregnant, but I almost bled to death. Dr. Bill did not tell me I was pregnant but did say I should think about not having more children. I told the doctor, after much questioning, that Douglas was a cruel heathen and I believed he might kill me and make it look like an accident. Douglas had told me several times that he could throw me in a well on his land and no one would ever find me. After that visit the doctor told both of us he would file a police report if anything like this happened again.

I didn't see Dr. Bill for about a year after that. Then, while visiting a friend at Self Memorial Hospital, I ran into the doctor leaving the hospital, and he stopped me, asking how things were going at home. I told him things were better and though our relationship as husband and wife had ended, we lived in the same house, hardly speaking, each going our separate ways. We talked for only a few minutes more and then, before he got into his car, he walked back to me and said, "Lady, you deserve better, please do something about your situation and don't wait, you are in extreme danger."

Later that the week, I received a call from Dr. Bill, and we agreed I should plan on taking back my life. I started seeing the doctor once a week and a lady from mental health who was a close friend of Dr. Bill also met with us for about three months. I was encouraged to leave Douglas and start a new life. After the three months ended I started working at a textile mill, but took time off to spend three hours a week with Dr. Bill. We developed a close relationship as lovers as well as friends.

At first we met at his office; later we met at different places, sometimes on a country road where we would not be seen. We often met at the Old Dysan Brick Yard, which had been closed for years. This building was located on Route Three a few miles out of the small textile mill town called Ninety Six, South Carolina. We sat on a wooden bench and talked, often ending in each other's arms, and several times we found ourselves inside one of the buildings removing our clothing quickly in our need for each other.

I learned that sex could be a beautiful experience when force was not an issue and no one was in control. At the age of twenty-nine I experienced my first orgasm in the arms of this kind, gentle man. I had three children, had never enjoyed sex, and had never felt love and respect was a part of sex. I remember crying for some time afterwards, and I had a difficult time explaining to Dr. Bill how I felt because this was something with which I was unfamiliar.

There was much discussion and analyzing, and we left the building knowing we would return soon or meet somewhere else to be together. Our fondness for each other was reaching a high peak, and we did nothing to restrict our need for each other. We swam in Lake Greenwood at night when I could leave my job early at the textile mill. (I kept a swimsuit at his office that he brought along with him.) Dr. Bill liked to lie in the tall grass near the lake and nap, while I swam. We both enjoyed these evenings, and he encouraged me to talk about Granny and the mountain people.

One night an incident occurred that kept us apart for several weeks. We were lying in the grass enjoying the closeness of two lovers when a man walked up and cleared his throat, then walked away quickly. At the time I was being kissed from head to toe, feeling I was in another world and almost at the point of never returning to the world I lived in. There were no houses on Lake Greenwood at the time, and we wondered where the man had come from.

Shortly after that, Emma Lucy Hault came to see me at the textile mill where we both worked and told me she was at the lake that night with a friend, and for me not to worry because their lips were sealed. Emma Lucy became a friend and remained so for years. The gentleman was one of Dr. Bill's patients who owned a grocery store in Ninety Six. I saw him several times during the summer months when taking the children to the lake. He always nodded his head and smiled. I wonder what he was thinking, and if he remembered my face.

The children soon grew tired of the lake and became bored, and I made arrangements for them to go to Virginia to visit my family for several weeks during the summer. The three Hault girls joined them, and Emma Lucy spent most of the summer in the country with me. She later moved to Washington with her family, and never returned to Ninety Six.

I spent most of those long summer days making plans to start a new life elsewhere. My sister, Mary, had asked me to come to Michigan to live with her. I didn't know where we would go at that time, but I knew that when I left, my daughters Sandy, Elaine and Melba would leave with me.

As Granny had so often stated, everything is going somewhere. I had arrived at a place in my life where I felt life was worthwhile, and my relationship with Dr. Bill continued for four years. In our long talks, I told him the many things that had affected my life and he in turn shared some most difficult times in his own life.

I respected and admired him so. Our friendship had turned in to a full-blown, special relationship, and I found out for the first time in my life what passion, respect, fulfillment and regard for another person is all about. This did not happen overnight, but the wounds were healing. I was beginning a transformation that helped me cope with life and freed me from the armor I had constructed around myself for protection. I was beginning to feel that I was a whole person. I had high self-esteem, thanks to Dr. Bill, who told me countless times that I was a lady. He called me "lady" when speaking to me ever since we met at the hospital when I was visiting a friend.

Dr. Bill had earlier told me he wanted to suggest something to me that would affect my future life. "If you continue living with Douglas you will have more children and this will discourage you in your plans to leave him. I know you love your children, but please allow me to speak to a colleague of mine, Dr. Snyder, a surgeon. He will tie your tubes to prevent further pregnancies. He says this can be reversed at any time if you wish to have more children. Please think about it and let me know the next time we meet." I was grateful for his advice and accepted the procedure.

After some time we realized how our relationship could affect his practice if we continued seeing each other. There was a lot at stake for both of us should we be discovered, and at last we agreed not to see each other alone again.

Some time later when he told me he was getting married, I wished him much happiness. I did send a card to him quite a bit later telling him I was doing well, that I had a new life, and thanking him for his kindness, but I did not give him my address. I just wanted to let him to know I had taken his advice.

CHAPTER 42

After Fourteen Years, I Left Douglas And Started A New Life

DURING THE ENTIRE time I was in South Carolina all those years, Connie, the lady who helped me get the textile mill job, also remained a close friend. Our friendship was helpful and supportive to both of us, as she too had married a man that was abusive. Having this common bond made our friendship stronger. Connie had three children and stayed in her troubled marriage until her husband died years later.

In the meantime, after the beating I got from tampering with Douglas' books, I found other ways to find trouble, or perhaps trouble found me. I was labeled a troublemaker in our community because of my interest in the people who were taken advantage of, most of whom were black.

One of our largest crops on the farm was cotton, and eighty percent was picked by hand. Each year when it came time for the cotton to be picked, the black children in the area were customarily kept out of school in order to pick. I was asked about my opinion at a group meeting regarding this action. I stated that I would refuse to take the children of our workers out of school to pick some landowner's cotton who had no intention of giving them one tenth of what was due them, and who had a well-laid plan to keep the tenants in debt to him in order to hold them so the cheating process could be continued from year to year.

The following week, many in our area attended a community meeting. However, yours truly failed to receive an invitation, but I got the message when a large cross was burned on our front lawn the same night! A number of spineless men wearing white robes and hiding behind masks stood against one lone woman with her three frightened children standing behind her, with dear Josephine crying in the bedroom closet, afraid not for her life but for mine. I took my three-year-old daughter in my arms and tried to quiet her. I was shaking not from fright but with hatred and disgust for the actions of these white-robed cowards. Before I stepped away from the upstairs window, I straightened my shoulders and screamed words that men like these were able to understand.

After this, we were refused the privilege of purchasing fertilizer in South Carolina and found it necessary to pay extra trucking fees from Georgia. I believe this added insult to Douglas' injury. His temper was short and his pride had been hurt, so he sulked alone while Josephine and I went about the business of caring for our home and children.

During the year 1950, I spoke to many persons of color and encouraged them to register to vote in the coming elections. This was not an easy task, because even though it was legal for "people of color" to vote at that time, the fear of retaliation caused many to refuse to register or even talk to me about the important matter of voting. When I knocked on doors, I often had a glimpse of a frightened face at the window. I was persistent, though, and soon had several adults ready to register in Ninety Six, Greenwood County, South Carolina,

I spoke to these people about the importance of voting, and did this knowing the risk of being an outcast. I knew also that my children would probably suffer because of my action. The KKK (Ku Klux Klan) was still active and the intimidating fear of these ungodly robed men was intense among poor white and black people alike.

Upon arriving at the registration station we were immediately turned away, and not one person was registered to vote. The authorities told me that day that I would never be able to vote in South Carolina again and I believed them.

Jennie, a lovely lady that lived within two miles of our home across a winding county road in a wooded area, came to see me one morning to inform me that her brother had not been seen for several days and she was afraid for him since he was one of the men I had encouraged to register to vote. I tried to reassure her that these men would not dare do anything to harm these people, telling her the law was on our side. Jennie went away not questioning me, but she looked very sad. I could tell she was fearful just as I was. We did not know what awaited us in days to come.

Jennie's brother never returned. A few people on Route 3 told of dogs bringing human bones to their yards and barn lots, but no investigation was ever conducted and nothing was ever done about this incident.

During all this time I had tried keeping in touch with Granny and Fern and Aunt Violet, and they had always answered my letters. I sent Granny money, but she always returned it, saying she didn't need anything she didn't already have, so I stopped after a bit, and the time lengthened between letters.

I had a tutor, Charles Fuller, whose instruction furthered my education. We spent hours studying, and after awhile he set up residence in our home. Sometimes we read through most of the night together, and Josephine often came into the dining room and insisted we retire, saying it was two or three o'clock in the morning.

I give credit for my enrollment in our small town's school to Mr. Fuller. who, at that time, worked for the Health Department. He had confidence in my ability and came out to my house and talked with me about the possibility of my attending nurse's training. He also arranged for me to talk with a lady at Self Memorial Hospital in Greenwood. She was instrumental in helping me get into school, and was a pillar of strength while I fought to stay there.

I worked very hard, but there was much crowding in my mind, and it appeared to my instructor that I was trying to show the other students up. I wasn't, but sometimes I did or said things without thinking that, according to the teacher, were utterly impossible for me to do or know given my present level of education. So I found myself holding back, trying hard not to do the things I knew I could do with little or no effort. It seemed many of the natural healing methods taught me by Granny were not appropriate in this atmosphere.

The first year was difficult, partly because of the children. Douglas seemed always to be angry and he often took it out on them. My home life constantly seemed to be on edge. As time passed, and with most of the so-called respectable people not thinking too highly of me, I knew that some day I would have to take my children and start a new life elsewhere.

My friend Sam had Granny's address and he had written a letter to her asking about me. Poor Fern, not knowing the ways of the world and the people who live in it, sent Sam's letter on to me. Sam was fearful the medical treatment I'd had in Augusta might affect my memory and wanted to know I was all right. Unfortunately, both Aunt Fern's and Sam's letters were discovered by Douglas.

I found this out a few months later when Douglas hired a private investigator to probe into Sam's life, and in doing so unearthed my multitude of sins and transgressions (my various marriages, relationships, and jobs). He flung them into my face in a fit of rage not fitting a nice Southern gentleman. He'd already suffered because of my actions, and now his pride was injured as well. He showed me all the material he had gathered, and it was enough to hang an innocent person, let alone a guilty one.

I tried to make him see that I had never done one thing to hurt him or our children and would never do so, but he was right in his assumption that I had lied to him, and he thought I could never be trusted.

Poor Sam. The hell I'd already inflicted upon him was enough for the lives of any ten men, and in the final analysis, was devastating not only to him but also to me and the only people I really loved, my three daughters.

I returned to school the following day, but my heart wasn't in it. I couldn't think, and came home early to find a lady there, a member of the school board. She was listening to my poor, mistreated husband's tale of woe, and she believed every word of it. I'm sure she inserted a few well-chosen tidbits of her own when she found his weren't exciting enough.

She spread her version of my story around our small town, which resulted in me being called into the office at school and being given a choice: I could quietly drop out, or I could be given a notice not to return. I accepted the latter. I was told I would be a bad influence on the students who came to school for the purpose of improving themselves. Of course I did not respect their judgment, but I had to accept it.

I tried to talk with my husband about this and about my whole life, to explain what I did and why, and to ask if he would be more understanding of what I'd been through, but he couldn't understand my feelings and refused to discuss it with me. My first thought was to run away, a thought I conveyed to him. He threatened to throw me into an old abandoned well on our property if I tried to take the children with me. He took my car, and as I then had no access to any money, I was forced to stay because I would not leave the children. Therefore, I played a waiting game.

Following this, for five years I labored with his field hands—literally. I went to the field early each morning and returned when it was no longer possible to see. This left me very little time to spend with my children. I am so thankful they were in Josephine's care.

The summer my oldest daughter Melba turned fourteen, I was so depressed that I decided to take my life. I planned this for two weeks. I drove Douglas' car and parked on a back road near Dysan, about six miles from Ninety-Six. I'd brought a large Irish potato in the car from our garden, and when I stopped the car and tried to put the potato into the exhaust pipe, it wouldn't fit! I used a large rock, striking the potato several times before I rammed it into the pipe. I started the car, wrapped myself in a blanket I'd brought, threw a pillow in the back seat, and settled down for my final sleep.

I lay awake for a long time, or so it seemed, but finally I began to feel sleepy and was experiencing a very peaceful feeling just before there came a pounding on the car door. In my drugged dreams I saw a face in the car window, and I awoke a bit later on a grassy mound with rough hands shaking me, slapping my face, calling out to me, "Why in the world would you do something like this?"

It took several hours for me to clear my head, and then I got to my feet and walked away, not stopping to thank this person for saving my life. I returned several hours later to retrieve the car.

I wasn't to feel the sweet sensation of death I had longed for and chosen. I was to live and despise my life and my day-to-day existence. But I eventually came to realize that my love for my daughters far outweighed my desire to die, and I then knew I would never try again to take my life, not ever! There was a reason for my being here. I was responsible for my three girls as well as myself. Whatever I was to do, I must do quickly and without regrets.

When I had taken all I could without experiencing a complete mental and physical breakdown, I sat down to write Granny a letter, the last she was ever to receive from me. I wrote of what my time with her had meant to me, and assured her that I loved her very much.

Then I sent Sam a night letter asking him for money after giving him a few details of how hard my life had been and that I needed to leave. Although we had not seen one another for years, this dear man immediately mailed me a certified cashier's check for $10,000, part of the proceeds earned by his colt whose mother's head I had held in my arms while she gave birth.

I knew that somewhere my husband had Granny's address. I prayed he would not get in touch with her nor hurt her by telling her of my past life. I knew he was capable of doing this.

I packed our clothes, and the children and I walked out the side door to wait for a taxi. While we were waiting, I looked back at the old house and started to think. My mind took me back to my first encounter with this house. First I had lived there as mistress of the house; next as a laborer in the field; now here I was, an unwanted, guilt-ridden person, who, thus far, had been unable to find herself. How much time had passed since I arrived! I counted the years, and I knew we all had paid dearly for the greed that possessed me from the time I set my heart on ownership of this property.

I made haste to depart before anything could detain me. Once we were safe in a nearby town, I began making plans to get as far away as we could, as quickly as we could. The following day I bought a second-hand automobile. We packed our belongings in the trunk and were ready to begin our journey. The clock was ticking away the hours and I was unable to sleep, so I sat out in the cool night air to think.

I was all alone one moment, and the next thing I knew, my husband was holding me in his arms and begging me not to leave! He promised me that things would be different if I returned home. He assured me he had never for one moment thought I'd been unfaithful, and we could rebuild our lives together.

I awoke the children and we returned to a house that seemed silent and forlorn.

Well, of course Douglas had not changed nor did he intend to, though he did not beat me as before. I'd have felt better if he had. Instead, he went for weeks without speaking to either our children or me.

One night he told Josephine he wouldn't be home till late. I noticed he had taken a box of shells from the gun cabinet, and I asked

PEARL K. MCCULLOUGH

Josephine if he was going hunting this time of night. I followed him to the barn and watched through a knothole as he pulled a large box from the harness room where he'd hidden it under some gear. When he finally left, I knew there was far more to this man's life than I had ever known about.

Douglas came home at about five a.m. I'd just drifted off to sleep, but awoke when Josephine shook me and told me he wanted to see me. I threw on a robe and went to the kitchen where he was having coffee. He rose to his feet, pulled out a chair, and asked me to sit down and talk. He told me he'd been thinking of our lives all night while out walking, and we must work together to organize our lives for the sake of the children.

I agreed, and he took my hand and we walked out into the morning light to visit his parents' grave located in the family cemetery a short distance from the house. When we reached the white iron fence and sat on a bench near the gate, he asked me to promise him on his mother's grave that nothing would ever come between us again. We walked back to the house after he had paid his respects to his parents. We met Josephine as we entered the front hall, and I heard my husband tell her to remember that he had not been out last night.

Later I questioned her, and she told me I had misunderstood, he had not said this, but knowing Josephine's fear, I doubted her veracity.

While we were having breakfast I asked, "Where were you last night?"

He answered, "In bed with you, and see that you don't forget it." His voice was as cold as a winter wind, but his blue eyes were half-smiling.

I learned from my oldest daughter when she arrived home from school that evening that a black man's house had been burned last night and several other homes of black people had been fired into because they had gone to register to vote and had to be stopped. Then I realized why my husband had his change of heart.

As soon as Douglas was out in the field the next day, I did what I thought was right in my heart. I went to the harness room, uncovered the box, and withdrew its contents: a white robe and mask and a bullwhip that had been missing from our trophy case for several years. This was my first knowledge that my husband was a member of the KKK, which had been responsible for so much suffering, agony, and even death of people who opposed them. I have always wondered if he played a part in the drama of that cross-burning on our lawn.

I presented the box as I'd found it to the local authorities in our town along with my story. I was asked to leave the premises before I was bodily removed, and was told they didn't need my kind of people there! I immediately returned home, now knowing with certainty what I must do.

I threw our clothes into bags and was ready to leave in one hour. I sent Josephine to the nearest tenant's house with a message; this was to protect her and get her out of the house. I then proceeded to soak the hall, dining room and kitchen with gasoline. I took an umbrella from the hall rack, ignited it, and threw it as far down the hall as possible, and I closed the door on that house I'd loved so much. I calmly walked to my car and, with my daughters, drove down the drive as usual. Before we were out of sight of the house I could see black clouds of smoke billowing from the structure. I felt in my heart that everyone had gotten their just desserts, including me.

The house would rest in its ashes. The garden would slowly and surely succumb to the vines and briars that nature provided, but what of me? Would my hatred become a flaming mass that would engulf me and those I loved before I could rest in my own ashes of self-destruction?

CHAPTER 43

My Move To A New Life

THE DIVORCE PROCEEDINGS gave me custody of the children. I also received four hundred acres of land, and Douglas was ordered to pay child support of $25 a month for each child, although that only lasted for a few months. Douglas' sister Ruth contacted my lawyer, the most severe attorney I could find, stating that she would be a witness for me regarding the cruelty she had witnessed several times by my husband to the children and me. Ruth and I had also met with Douglas, telling him of our plans to expose his dishonesty to people of color and his association with the KKK. Given all this, he did not contest the divorce, so Ruth was not called to testify. My attorney sold the land for me, and this money took my daughters and me to California to begin a new life.

Melba, my oldest daughter, went to Michigan to live with my sister, and Sandy and Tobie, my two youngest daughters, stayed with me. I enrolled them in school and began looking for work, and within a few days I found work at the Carmel Convalescent Hospital in Carmel. I also enrolled in a Nursing Aide Program, taking every course I could find on caring for the aging.

Most of the time I worked six or seven days a week, and in the evenings I walked downtown Monterey, taking in the many sights and sounds of the busy, bubbling city that was always intriguing to me.

I noticed that many of the girls hanging out on the streets in downtown Monterey were not much different from the ones I'd known in Harlan, Kentucky. Realizing they were women of the night encouraged me to get closer to them in an effort to help them in some way. I ended up spending much of my money buying breakfast for this girl or that one at a small cafe several days a month. After some time, with the help of a friend, Alice Greenwood, I established an employment agency as a non-profit organization in an effort to assist these young girls in reshaping their lives.

Alice introduced me to Rev. Dean Hendricks, pastor of his church, and we spent hours talking with other members of the church, with the end result that my employment agency became an outreach program under the sheltering umbrella of the church ministry and the church would fund the agency.

Through this program, many girls were able to return home to their parents, while others found long-term employment. Lives were changed because of the love and compassion shown by the people of the church. To this day, I still hear from some of the girls I assisted and encouraged.

All this became a springboard for many other projects I either started myself or became involved in. One such project was Operation Fishnet, a program developed to help seniors stay in their homes as long as possible with care given by family and friends. We found "live ins" when possible, and paid them a small fee plus room and board. Volunteers could be incorporated into this type of service, sometimes church members. The response from the public was outstanding, and our outreach program was extended.

I started a Residential Care Home for the elderly and this business grew rapidly, expanding into four separate homes.

I also began a Community Awareness program in the 70s, sponsored by my Residential Care Homes. This radio talk program was a community program in which hospital, home care nurses, doctors and others could be involved. I did interviews, set up the one-hour program, and tried to keep the talk flowing between organizations as we made progress towards awareness in our community. This became quite a successful and rewarding endeavor.

My work in prisons allowed me to touch the lives of others with outstretched hands and an open heart, and I will always remember the time spent as a volunteer for the church.

A true blessing was being the founding president of Yellow Brick Road, a local and successful, rather upscale thrift shop still going strong today, and from this work I received so much more than I could ever give.

In this book, *A Mended Vessel*, I have tried to protect the innocent and the not so innocent by using fictitious names, while offering encouragement to women to not accept defeat, to know that there is strength within, and to help get through difficult times. Never stop trying. Always love yourself, and then you will be able to love others so that they can accept and love you in return.

CHAPTER 44

Answer To An
Age-Old Question

MANY YEARS LATER, when I was 60, my brother Edd agreed to go with me to Meadow Fork, North Carolina, to seek out Granny's final resting place. We found the cemetery after stopping in Hot Springs and inquiring about our family history. We arrived late in the afternoon after having lunch at a small place near South Fork.

We found ourselves lingering in the cemetery a good part of the afternoon, pulling weeds and talking. My brother stated, "You must have loved her a lot." That was the understatement of the year! I explained, "She taught me more in a few years than I could have learned in several lifetimes."

As we were leaving the cemetery, my eyes froze on the name on a headstone nearby. My heart seemed to burst in my chest. On the headstone was a picture of the young man that had caused me so many years of heartache and grief following his cruel act on a cold, gray afternoon in my grandmother's barn. That young man had taken away the pleasures the beautiful mountains had given a young girl—who had been stabbed not once but twice with the sword of sexual reality.

"How could this be?" I asked myself, and tried to regain my composure. "Why now, when I feel that I have recovered, forgiven, and almost erased that episode from my memory?"

I found it difficult to walk to the car, and I cried for some time, not saying anything to Edd. He allowed me time to regain control of myself, and then asked quietly if I wanted to talk about anything.

"No," I answered, "no, I do not." We never referred to that again.

I returned to California and continued on with my daily life. The wound that had been reopened, and the pain and terrible dreams that had tortured me for so many years, began to appear night after night. The name on the headstone had been indelibly stamped in my mind as if by a searing branding iron. I could see it so clearly and felt the pain and total devastation as if the violation was being relived all over again.

I found solace and comfort only in my church and through my wonderful doctor who has helped me these many years. The struggle has been long and never easy, but I'm so thankful I was finally able to forgive, if not to forget.

CHAPTER 45

My Happy Ending

IN 1989 WHILE attending a retired officers' dinner in Carmel, California, I was introduced by mutual friends to Mack McCullough, a man who would have a special place in my heart and my life. His wife had recently died during the time of the California Earthquake in October that year.

We did not see each other for some time following that evening, and then, about a year later, he called and asked me if I would have dinner with him, and I agreed. We talked for hours that night and found that we had a lot in common.

Over a two-year period we agreed there would be no secrets between us, and after many long hours of talking we realized that our relationship was most important. The word "marriage" had surfaced, and we wanted to be sure that our lives together would be permanent and rewarding.

At one of our meetings I handed Mack a synopsis of *A Mended Vessel*, asked him to read it in its entirety, and then talk to me. He was back in three hours and took me in his arms. We were both weeping as he said, "Well, nothing has changed."

After several more dinners, walks on the beach, and going to meet Mack's family in Oklahoma, I knew we were getting serious. At seventy years of age, however, I was not at all sure that this was what I wanted. I still owned a business and enjoyed my life just as it was. The word marriage had surfaced again and I found myself with recurring fears of being hurt or perhaps hurting this kind, gentle giant of a man. I knew I could be heartless if threats of physical or mental abuse were ever indicated in our relationship.

My next step was not easy for me, but it was necessary. I wanted so much to be honest with myself and with my future husband. Mack wanted us to spend more time together and he encouraged me to retire, so I agreed and closed the last of several assisted care homes I owned, as well as the nursing registry and employment agency, and we traveled for several years.

I so wanted to finish this book that I had started fifty years earlier. I had bits and pieces of my story stowed away in tins and boxes now yellowed with age, stained with many tears, and waiting to be put together as one would a jigsaw puzzle—choosing the edges, the center, the background, and the masses of color, bold and daring, the grays, the raw reds—that splashed and slashed my life as well as others. All this, tinted with the green color of high mountains, the shades of mist on a frosty morning, the transparency of a cool, enticing waterfall, the color of leaves as they dance in graceful motion in the breeze. Is this the end, or the beginning of a new life?

I am happy to say a new life began that day. Mack and I have now been husband and wife for sixteen years and know that we will spend the rest of our lives together.

PEARL K. MCCULLOUGH, now eighty-six years of age, is a first time writer. She was born in the Great Smoky Mountains of North Carolina, and moved to Tom's Creek, Virginia at the age of two months. There she lived until her mother died during the Great Depression. She later relocated with her family to a small mining village near St. Charles, Virginia. This story, *A Mended Vessel*, is a true recounting of her early life during which she survived traumas and difficulties that not many people could have overcome.

After breaking the pattern of abuse and trouble she experienced for so many years, Pearl moved to California at the age of thirty-nine. Here she has owned and operated four convalescence homes in Carmel over a period of twenty-five years; she has taken over twenty-seven foster children into her home; was Director of Operation Fishnet; was the Founding President of The Yellow Brick Road, an enormously successful high-end benefit shop; and did volunteer work at a local prison. She also worked with "'women of the night" and emceed a radio talk show focusing on community awareness.

Pearl is a self-educated woman who received some formal education later in life. She now lives in Carmel, California with Mack, her husband of sixteen years, and their beloved poodle, Touché.

Toby Elaine   2 yrs
Sandra Sue   4 yrs
Melba Ruth   6 yrs
in one of our cornfields in SC

My Granny Alice Gregory
in front of her vegetable garden

Get Published, Inc!
Thorofare, NJ 08086
09November 2009
BA2009249